Arabian Business & Cultural Guide

Your guide to do's and don'ts in the Arabian culture & market

By Mohammad Al-Sabt

Copyright, Legal Notice and Disclaimer:

Dedicated to understanding, tolerance and to bridging the distances and the differences

Thank You

I would like to thank my wife & family for the great help and support they have given me throughout the years.

A special thank you goes to my editor, Andrea Reich and to my first international trade mentor, Tony Livoti

Introduction

So many times I have heard the same complaint from an American exporter or an international sales executive that he or she is tired of providing quotations and catalogs to prospective Arabian clients without any progress in their business or even a single sale. They need to know that they are on the right track and even if it takes 6 or even 12 months to receive the first order, it is worth it because after that they are guaranteed the Arabian client for a long time.

On many occasions I have had a discussion with an American exporter and counted several opinions, sentences, and gestures that, if they had been in a meeting with an Arabian businessman, they would have failed completely before they even had a chance to introduce their service or product.

Having a salable product and a good marketing effort is not enough to succeed in the Arabian market. You need to study the culture of that market and apply your knowledge in all of your business plans.

It is very important to understand that the guidance and advice given in this book are meant to shed some understanding on the Arabian business culture and hopefully to help you, the reader, in succeeding in your business ventures. It is not meant to convey that one culture is superior or better than another.

When you are determined to succeed in your international business or even to effectively communicate with a foreign client, you have to be open-minded, observant and respect the existing differences.

In my opinion, sometimes it is not a compromise to your true beliefs when you adjust your regular behavior to avoid insulting or discomforting your foreign business partner or host. It might be a sign of arrogance and a closed mind to actually be aware of the differences and choose not to utilize that knowledge.

After reading this book, I would like to invite you to feel free to contact me with any comments, questions or suggestions you might have. I will appreciate very much your sharing with me (and possibly with others in next editions of this book) your experiences with the Arabian business cultures. Anyone who wants to get involved in international trading should realize the fact that he or she will be acting as a mediator between two cultures, bringing the buyer and the seller to a comfortable common ground where both of them communicate successfully and profitably.

Table of Contents

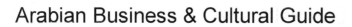

Chapter 1
Rules Of Thumb

Information sources

My family was so worried about me going to the United States in 1989 to get my master's degree in computer science. They were worried that I would get killed because they thought that at every corner in the United States there lurks a criminal or an earthquake. Well, I don't blame them. The only images they saw about the US were from TV movies and the news which were mostly filled with violence, earthquakes, floods, etc. That was funny though. Why? Because in the US I was asked many times how it felt to come from a violence filled region, and if I was used to the sound of bombs and guns going off every day. My family and the people I met in the US each thought they were living in a safer environment than the other. Of course, the people who asked me had the same source my family had, the news, which by definition means something worthy of mentioning like a disaster, war and violence . Have you ever heard on the news that things today are going smooth and there are no problems!

When I used to live in California, every time my family saw a news report about a flood or an earthquake, they would call me to see if I was safe even if the news was from Florida! To them the news included all of the United States. Of course, I ended up giving my family a USA map so they could locate the distance between where I live and what was reported on the news. It worked.

This illustrates that people have the same sources for news and most likely might have the same conclusion; many countries are grouped into one single understanding and state of mind which can't be any further from the truth. If you are planning to do business or visit the Arabian states or any part of the Middle East, remember that your information sources may not yield a complete understanding of the environment and the culture.

In this book, you will be introduced to many sides of the Arabian culture that might appear not to be directly related to doing business. Remember that a significant percentage of the business decision process is related to the person making the decision; therefore, the more you understand the person, the better your chance of communicating effectively.

Priority List

The more you know about your prospective client's culture, the better your presentation and correspondence will be. This is especially true when dealing with the Arabian market. One very important aspect of the Arabian culture that you will see repeated in many ways in this book is that maximum financial profit "is not" the top priority. At the top of the priority list comes honor, reputation, and family ties. In the previous sentence I have placed a quotation mark around "is not" so you can substitute it with "might not be". As you know, people of the same culture are still different individuals and might have a different priority list in their life.

Business is not business

The expression "Business Is Business" does not apply to the Arabian market culture. Pure profit that might be obtained causing a conflict to the higher items on the priority list is not really an incentive to a business decision. The lesson here is that business in the Arabian culture falls within the parameter of measuring success to be the success that is achieved without endangering ones honor, reputation, or family ties.

Communication network

Businesses are usually run by and awarded to family members, friends and relatives. Relationship ties are very strong and one's family includes not only his immediate relatives, but extends to his distant relatives, tribe members, friends and neighbors. For that reason the communication speed is fast, the depth effectiveness is strong and the distribution channel is big.

Don't be surprised if your very close relationship with an Arabian businessman has grown your business base and diversity tremendously. At the same time, the bad business or experience someone has incurred will be known by many. You can get a sense that businesses are influenced by the intricate human relations and cultural values.

A few years ago while I was on a business trip to Saudi Arabia, I heard a story on several occasions from different sources .It was about an Arabian businessman who operated a very successful and profitable exporting company from Germany for four years. He was exporting German-made products to his primary market, the Arabian countries. This market made him a millionaire, but it seems that with time and success he underestimated the network to which he was selling. He started raising his commissions for some of his clients, with the false excuse that the cost of the goods was increasing, while at the same time he supplied others at the regular price. He also made promises to some of his clients that he did not keep. It did not take too long until everyone realized what he was doing and that was the end of his business in that market.

A friend of mine who is a very successful Arabian businessman was the middleman between a department in an Arabian defense ministry and an American manufacturer. My friend had a verbal agreement with the American company for a set commission when the deal was completed. In advanced stages of negotiations, the American company was corresponding directly with all parties involved including the end buyer. After 8 months of hard work on the deal, the American company started ignoring the middleman. After many persistent calls and fax messages by my friend, the American company responded with a fax message promising him with a commission that was lower than what was originally agreed. My friend simply informed his friends at the government office of this development, started corresponding with another source, and guaranteed that this company will never do business in his country.

Underestimating the power of communication in the Arabian market will drive you out of business in that region. On the other hand, this communication power will increase your business tremendously when you show that you are consistent, honest, and trustworthy. Although tides of change did not spare any culture or region, still a good percentage of the business in the Arabian world is done by a handshake.

At the heart of the Arabian culture lies an understanding that one's life mission and meaning is to be unselfish, unattached to the material life, and devoted to his family. The culture encourages people to have sincere enjoyment in serving and helping others. The true reward one is seeking is to be loved, appreciated, and considered reputable by all. Being generous, honest, respectful, and loyal are the values one is encouraged to live by.

International trade market

The fact that the Arabian countries do not manufacture most of the goods they consume and use, means that a need always existed to import. Although the governments of this region are trying to encourage national manufacturing, the lack of raw materials is a hindrance. Therefore, exports to the Arabian market are continually needed. The dependence on imports coming from all around the world should give you an indication that they are very knowledgeable about the world markets, goods quality, variations, and prices.

The Arabian businessman is very educated and well traveled. Prior to oil discovery, Arabs built their own ships sailing the seas and traveled with their camels through the deserts to trade with distant countries. Oil discovery enabled the Arabian states to use their extensive international trading experience to successfully trade all over the world.

Chapter 2
Communication Etiquette

The Arabian culture contains very detail oriented traditions and etiquette covering almost every facet of their life. The best way to learn more about a culture is to observe, observe, and observe. Of course, if you are primarily dealing with another culture through the phone, the mail, or the fax machine, you have limited access to observe the way they interact with each other. I have divided the communication etiquette into three sections: written communication, verbal communication, and non-verbal communication.

Written Communication

Choice of words

Arabs use certain words in their business correspondence that convey respect and place a human touch in their business. The following are some words which are often used:

- Kind : Thank you for your kind cooperation, we would like to receive your kind quote, we have received your kind message, kindly quote us the following.
- Honor : It is our honor to supply your company with the following information, thank you for giving us the honor of quoting you, it is an honor to serve your company.

Other words that will also create a favorable impression for your correspondence are: appreciate consideration, help and the like. Although you will not find any difficulty in communicating using the English language, you should use short clear sentences and avoid using words that are considered slang.

The main idea is to use your correspondence to convey more than the subject under discussion. Use your correspondence to convey the human side of your personality. On many occasions, I have used a fax cover sheet which contains a humorous cartoon to convey the message that I am sorry for the delay in our reply or a message informing them that we need their help, etc. A number of my Arabian clients have asked where to get these fax cover sheets and expressed that they enjoy them. I have even used humorous cartoon fax messages to remind some of our clients that we are still seeking their business. It worked every time. Arabs in general are very humorous and appreciate the human touch in their business. A warning here is that what might be humorous to you might not be to them. Make sure that your humor is a conservative one. In different parts of this book you will be introduced to some advertising and marketing guidelines which you can apply here.

Use of Arabic words

Another good tool to maximize the effectiveness of your correspondence and marketing efforts is to include a translation in Arabic. This is not necessary because English is understood, but it will make your message distinguished, attracts more attention and better response, and creates a special connection between your business and the targeted

client. To gain the positive effect of using Arabic in your correspondence, I have provided some Arabic sentences (next page) and their approximate English translation (below) that you can incorporate into your messages and letters. Feel free to photocopy or scan these sentences: We need your kind help.
Thank you for your cooperation.

1. Greetings to all
2. It is our pleasure to do business with you
3. Happy new year
4. Thank you for your kind order
5. We appreciate your trust in us
6. Enclosed is the quotation you have kindly requested
7. It is our pleasure to serve you
8. Urgent
9. Enclosed is the information you have requested
10. Important

It is very helpful to provide your clients with literature that is produced in their own language, especially if the literature will be passed by your overseas partners to their customers. If you intend on using a translation service provider, be sure that they fully understand the targeted language, audience and market. Producing a word by word translation of your current local product literature will not necessarily prove to be an effective equivalent of the original and in some cases might yield the opposite of your intended message. Every market has its own marketing and advertising rules and every audience is approached differently. I am sure that you have heard about some companies resulting to changing the name of their products when introduced to a foreign market because an exact translation proved to be ineffective or in some cases offensive.

(1) نحتاج لمساعدتكم الكريمة

(2) شكرا على تعاونكم الكريم

(3) تحية طيبة للجميع

(4) يسعدنا التعامل معكم

(5) كل عام وأنتم بخير

(6) شكرا لكم على طلبكم الكريم

(7) نحن نقدر ثقتكم بنا

(8) مرفق التسعيرة التي تكرمتم بطلبها

(9) تسعدنا خدمتكم

(10) مستعجل

(11) مرفق المعلومات التي طلبتموها

Verbal Communication

The same guidelines for written communication apply here with more emphasis on speaking simple, clear English with no slang. Many Arabian businessmen and businesswomen have high education degrees from the United States, Britain, France and other countries, and they are very fluent in a second or even a third language. A good rule though is to assume that they are not fluent in your native language.

Subjects to avoid

Avoid discussing certain issues that might cause conflict or discomfort to your Arabian listener. Some feel very strongly about discussions of politics, religion, history, and culture. On the other hand, you will find others who enjoy such discussions. A good rule is to avoid these subjects unless you have a very good relationship with your business partner or you are interested in learning more about a subject.

Avoid discussions and humor about sex, especially in a mixed gender setting. This subject is considered very private and only talked or joked about among long time friends of the same gender. In a mixed gender setting, just hinting about anything related to sex is considered very offensive and will put everyone in a very awkward situation.

Private issues

Although Arabs are approachable, friendly, and humorous, there are issues that are kept private. They rarely talk about their family or spousal problems even with their close friends or relatives.

A year ago I connected an American manufacturer with an Arabian importer, and I did not ask for a fee because it was a favor for a friend. I simply provided both of them with the information needed to initiate the correspondence. A month later the Arabian importer contacted me asking me to be the middleman between his company and the American manufacturer. I was puzzled, for there seemed to be no real need for my services. It turned out that the American manufacturer had mentioned to the Saudi importer some personal problems that he was facing at home. The American manufacturer was feeling comfortable with his Arabian partner and he saw no problem with talking about this subject. They were sharing stories about traveling, doing business, and many other issues. The Arabian importer felt awkward and embarrassed but he did not want to cut the communication, and that's why I was invited to be in the middle.

Criticism

Another aspect of communication that Arabs keep private is criticism. If there is a need to deliver criticism to an individual, it is always done one on one, not in the presence of others. This is done to protect the dignity of the criticized person and to ensure that criticism will have a better chance of being accepted in a constructive manner. Criticism is geared towered correcting a situation, not toward humiliating the criticized person, and that's why it is a private communication.

Greeting etiquette

When Arabs meet each other they take their time in the greeting process. They inquire about how things are going, if everything is well, etc. They will even ask about the status of a matter you mentioned the last time you met with them. Frequently the questions will not be related to the business relationship. It is a tradition intended to show sincere interest in you as a human being, and an expression of brotherhood and friendship. You should take time to answer the inquiries about yourself and at the same time ask about their well being in return.

In some situations there might be a tendency to try to make as many contacts as possible; this might cause you not to pay attention to the greeting tradition or to cut it short. That might be considered rude and it could appear that you are not interested in gaining the person's business. Your objective on these occasions is to make solid contacts, not to distribute your business card to everyone. Know that the more interest you show about the person you have just met, the better chance you will have to win their business. So take your time in the greeting process; it is part of successful marketing behavior in the Arabian world.

Invitations

Arabs are known to be very generous. It is part of their culture and an important aspect of their personality. If you are meeting with an Arabian businessman in his office or in a trade show and there is mutual interest in becoming business partners, you will probably be invited to dinner or lunch even if you have already discussed and agreed on the business relationship. You might not feel that this step is necessary at this stage or think that he was trying to be polite and friendly. Know that the invitation is part of the tradition and a duty they have to fulfill. It is a very good opportunity for you to develop a strong relationship with your prospective Arabian client.

As I have explained before, the concept "Business Is Business" does not apply in the Arabian market. Arabs prefer to do business with someone after they have developed a good friendship. The concept is, let's be friends and then we will do business for a long time. These dinner or lunch invitations are your golden chance to develop a friendship. It is also appropriate for you extend an invitation to them.

There are some fine points of etiquette that accompany the invitation. Let's assume that your Arabian business partner has just placed an invitation to you and you have replied that due to time limits you can't take him up on his generous offer. He will reconfirm his invitation by accommodating your time constraints and discussing the possibility of having lunch instead of dinner. The repeated questions by your prospective Arabian business partner might seem to be an invasion of your privacy, but it is simply a sincere way of showing that you are important to him. All of these efforts are genuine and your Arabian business partner is proving to you that he is serious about his invitation.

It is also a good idea that you ensure that the one who placed an invitation was not only trying to fulfill his traditional duty to place it, but also, the invitation is in no contradiction with his schedule. This might sound to you as a confusing situation, but you can sort through it by gently not accepting the invitation at the beginning until persistence is showing.

Should you accept all invitations? It is preferable to do so but it might not be possible because of time constraints or previous engagements. What is the best way to turn down an invitation? By giving a valid reason why you can't accept and by assuring that you will be delighted and honored to do it some other time.

When to start business discussions?

It is a good idea once you are present at the office of your prospective Arabian business partner or at the dinner table of your host, not to open discussions about business matters until he does so. Let him ease into the subject after both of you have finished the greeting process and confirmed to each other that you place the human relationship before material things like business details.

The use of Arabic words and sentences

It is a good idea to use some simple Arabic words and sentences in your interactions. It shows that you are a perceptive person and someone who wants to get closer to them. The following are some selected words and simple sentences that you might want to use:

In English	Arabic Pronunciation
Good Morning	Sabahlekhair
Good Afternoon	Masa'elkhair
Good Bye	Maa'salamah
Tomorrow	Gadan / Boukrah
Today	El'youm
In the morning	Sabahan
In the afternoon	Ma'ssa'an
Mr.	El'sayeed
Mrs.	El'sayeedah
Miss	El'aanesah
My name is	Esmee
What is your name	Maa-essmok
Its an honor	Tasher'rafna
Yes	Na'am
No	Laa
Thank you	Shoukrann
Please	Lo Samaht
Excuse me	Af-One
Welcome	Ahlan Wasahlan
It's my pleasure	Ues'ednee
Meeting	Edge-T-Ma'a
How are you doing	Kai'fa Haloukah

In English	Arabic Pronunciation
Come on in	Ta-Fa-Thell
Urgent	Mustajell
Important	Mo-hem
Thank you for your generosity	Shoukrann-Ala- Karamekum
I am sorry	Ana-Asef

Non-Verbal Communication

Non-verbal communication refers to body movements and positions. As with written and verbal communication, non-verbal communication can be used to convey respect, honor, and friendliness, among other things.

Greeting etiquette

Once you are in an Arabian country, you will notice that men greet each other with a handshake, coupled with a kiss or two on both sides of the cheeks if they have not seen each other for some time. If one of them is an old man and they have a family tie, or if the younger man has a great deal of respect for the older man, the younger man might kiss the forehead or the tip of the nose of the older man instead of his cheeks. The reason for kissing the tip of the nose or the forehead is because these parts are the highest points in the face and kissing them represents high respect. The tip of the nose and the forehead are considered a representation of dignity. If you are not an Arabian, this greeting tradition does not apply to you; a handshake is appropriate.

The right hand rule

There is a very general rule that applies to handshaking, eating, giving, and receiving. You always should use the right hand. It is another sign of respect and an old part of the Arabian culture. Never use the left hand when doing these things unless, of course, the item you are handling is heavy. Also, when handing someone an item like papers or money, be sure that it goes hand to hand and avoid placing it or throwing it on the table.

Position of body

When sitting, avoid positioning the sole of your foot or shoe in the direction of someone's body, especially in the direction of his or her face. This is considered insulting; the reasoning behind it is that the sole of the foot is the lowest part of the body that touches the ground.

Almost every Arabian house has a guests gathering room called "Dewaniah" or "Majless". All Dewaniahs are similar in that the seats are placed in a circular shape. This design ensures that every attendant in the Dewaniah is facing the front of everyone else. Standing or sitting, Arabs always try to avoid turning their back to anyone as a sign of respect.

Non-verbal signs of respect

Another tradition that is performed to show respect to others is that when someone enters an office or a Dewaniah, others already seated there will stand up to greet the new arrival. Greeting visitors while sitting is considered arrogant and disrespectful.

Lets say a group of Arabians were walking together towered a door. The sequence in which everyone enters through the door has its own etiquette. The general rule is the person on your right has the right to go before you. If you are the guest or there is someone who is elderly, everyone will wait until the guest or the elderly person enters first. Arabs always exhibit a great deal of respect and honor to their elderly and to their guests. Another way of exhibiting respect to the elderly is that when people are standing in a line, such as in front of the post office or a bakery, everyone will invite the elderly person to go in front of him. A person's age will determine the set of etiquette he is entitled to and the set of etiquette he must perform in the Arabian world.

Touching as a sign of closeness and friendship

A friend of mine who is an Arabian businessman frequently attends international exhibits all over the world. He had formed a friendship with one of his American business partners who attend these shows as an exhibitor. At one of the shows, while both of them were joking and laughing, my Arabian friend tried to hold the hand of his American friend. The American businessman reacted with shock and withdrew. My friend immediately apologized to his American partner and explained to him that what he tried to do is a part of his culture in expressing close friendship.

Men in the Arabian world show closeness and friendship to each other by sometimes holding hands for a brief time when they are talking, walking, or escorting each other. They also pat each other on the back to express the same message. Some visitors to the Arabian world might feel uncomfortable with this expression, but it is important to know the meaning behind it. This closeness is only exhibited to people whom they have known for a long period of time and with whom they have a very close friendship.

If an Arabian client of yours expresses his appreciation of your friendship by holding your hand, it is a good idea not to withdraw or distance yourself abruptly. This action might cause a great deal of embarrassment to him, thinking that he had caused you discomfort.

Acknowledgment

When you enter your client's office or house or accidentally meet him somewhere, you should acknowledge everyone present at the meeting place or anyone escorting him by introducing yourself and greeting them by shaking their hands. It is rude not to acknowledge everyone present even if your meeting was for a very short period. Also when departing, you should express your pleasure of meeting everyone.

Chapter 3
Getting Down To Business

Before The Meeting

Work hours

For the most part, the GCC countries are a desert. Summer, with its extreme heat (up to 50C or 122F), sand storms, and humidity, runs from June to September. Winter, with its cool weather and occasional rainfall, runs from December to February. Autumn comes in October and November. Spring runs from March to May. Work hours are usually set to avoid the most intense heat during the day.

Most businesses have two daily working periods. The morning period lasts from 8:00am/9:00am until 1:30pm/2:30pm. The afternoon period is from 4:00pm/5:00pm until 8:00pm/9:00pm. In the hours between the two working periods, people usually go to their homes, have lunch, and take a nap. The hot weather is the determining factor behind this habit; if you live there you will appreciate this resting time. On Friday, which is a religious day to Muslims, the majority of businesses close (except for shops of course).

Ramadan

All the Arabian countries observe the fasting month "Ramadan", which is a very holy time in the Islam religion. During this month, drinking and eating (even smoking) is only done between sunset and sunrise. The beginning and the end of Ramadan is determined according to the Islamic calendar which is based on lunar sightings. The Islamic calendar contains 350 days a year.

During Ramadan, work hours might change in some Arabian countries. For example, the daily work hours may be from 10:00am until 1:30pm and from 7:00pm until 11:00pm during Ramadan. Because of the great religious importance of this fasting month, most people are in a worship mode and socialize with each other more. Business tends to slow down during Ramadan.

Slow business times

During the hottest summer months, July through August, most people in the GCC region vacation abroad to escape extreme heat and sand storms. You might notice that business slows down during the summer and then picks up by the beginning of September.

This knowledge is useful when planning a business trip. Also, you can understand why your Arabian clients have scaled down their business with you or are slower than usual in responding to your communication.

Setting up appointments

Sometimes when trying to set up meeting dates with your clients you will find that their answer is something like "Whenever you are in the area, give us a call". Don't interpret this as a sign of lack of interest in your business. It is equal to an answer that sets a specific date and time. Remember that business is done differently in that region. I prefer to describe it as a very relaxed and flexible system.If you will be meeting with the business owner or key decision maker, the hosting company might suggest the afternoon period. The reason for this is that some business owners work in a government office during the morning period and manage their businesses in the afternoon.

Let your clients know in advance that you will be visiting them and ask them to inform you what they might need before the meeting (catalogs, samples, prices, shipping costs, etc.). This way they will have enough time to evaluate the product and you have contributed to speeding up negotiations in an acceptable manner. Once you are meeting with them, it is a very good chance to ask for their feedback. Unless your product is one of a kind, they most likely have compared it with its competitors and they will use the information to discuss pricing.

Meeting length and punctuality

When you are setting up appointments, take into account that the meeting most likely will take longer than you expected. It is advisable to set at maximum two appointments in the same working period (for the morning period or the afternoon period). If you want to ensure enough time for every client you will meet, you should schedule one appointment for each working period. Some meetings might take up to 3 hours, where you will be introduced to the company management and taken on a tour.

Punctuality in set appointments is not a very high priority in many cases. The meeting that is scheduled for 4:30 PM might not start until 5:00 or even 5:30 PM. So if you show up in your client's office on time and wait 10 to 25 minutes to see your host, don't be surprised or show annoyance; it is a part of the relaxed pace of life in the Arabian world and does not mean that the appointment is not important.

As I mentioned before, in an Arabian's priority list in life, business comes below family and social duties. Everyone has a responsibility toward his family, relatives, and friends. Because of that, it is normal and sometimes a must for someone to re-arrange his business schedule (including meetings) in order to attend to an unexpected family or social duty. This does not indicate that previously arranged appointments are not respected but that other things are more important at that time.

Dress code

Arabs are mostly conservative in their way of dressing. If you are a man, avoid wearing earrings or other jewelry because it might distract the attention of your listeners from the main issue at hand. If you are a woman, it is preferable to wear a long dress or a jacket with a long skirt. Furthermore, both men and women should avoid wearing clothes with very loud colors.

The Meeting

Ask your host or hotel information desk about the time it will take you to get to your meeting destination so you can arrive on time. In some Arabian countries you will find that drivers don't comply with traffic laws and in others drivers are very courteous. Use taxi services; this way you will be sure to arrive at your destination very comfortably and without additional stress.

When to start and when to end the meeting

When you are seated in your prospective client's office, don't start discussing business until your host opens the subject. At the beginning, there will be greeting words and talk about other than business matters. Even by the end of the meeting, when business discussions are over, your host may go back talking about non-business subjects. When there is a longer than usual silence, that is your cue that it is time to leave.

Take notes

When business discussions start, it is a good idea to take notes. Information will include your prospective client's current needs, what they are looking for, problems they have faced before, experiences they had before with certain products, who are their suppliers, how do they do business, etc. The information given to you, even quotation requests, might not be available in a written form and that's why it is important that you take notes. In my business meetings with my Arabian clients, I always listen carefully and take notes. These meetings are very valuable sources for information about your market. You will find that your Arabian host is generous with the amount of information he gives to you.

Interruptions

Expect to have your meeting interrupted many times by people visiting your host, employees needing approval or a signature, and incoming phone calls. These interruptions do not mean that they are not interested in your business; it is just the business atmosphere there. You should realize it is an informal relaxed setting and that's how you should be, relaxed and not bothered or discouraged by having to repeat some of the ideas or subjects you were discussing before the interruption.

Muslims pray 5 times daily. Each prayer lasts for about 15 minutes: at dawn, midday, mid-afternoon, sunset, and nightfall. Prayers are usually held at Islamic worship places called "Mosques". Your host might interrupt the meeting for a prayer held in his company or a nearby Mosque.

Observe who is meeting with you

In some cases, you will find that you are meeting with two representatives of your host company. One of them is locally dressed and mostly listening, asking very few questions. The other representative is not locally dressed and is the one asking most of the questions. Most likely, the locally dressed person is the decision maker and the other person handles the technical side of the issues. Pay attention to both and talk to both when answering questions or making offers.

Pressure sales tactics

Do not use pressure sales tactics or deadlines. Exhibiting that you want to close the deal fast or make the sale in an urgent way, even when using incentives, might lead your efforts in the opposite direction and your offers will be refused eventually. Pressure sales tactics are viewed as signs of a bad deal and raise the flag of suspicion about what you are selling.

Price negotiations

Expect to negotiate on prices and fees charged for your products or services. Arabs are tough and experienced negotiators, but nevertheless try to reach a middle ground when they are very interested in the product under negotiation. Try to maintain your composure and not get upset. Price negotiations are performed in a friendly and relaxed atmosphere. It is better not to show annoyance or tension.

During your visit to your prospective client's country, check the market if possible and compare your product quality, specifications, and prices with comparable products on the market. This way you will know if your prices are competitive. Arrive at your destination two days before any meeting; use the extra time to collect valuable information by checking the market and researching business information that you can find in libraries, bookstores, and by reading local newspapers. English editions are available for a number of local newspapers.

Rejections

Arabs always try to ensure that their guests are very comfortable and treated with respect and friendliness; they avoid directly rejecting offers and invitations because it might cause discomfort to their guests and hence to them. So, rejection of an offer is done in a very subtle way. Your Arabian business host might ask for more time to study the subject or promise to keep your services on file for future needs. A number of American business people complained to me that they did not get results from their Arabian host or the Arabian businessman they met in a trade show, although these Arabian businessmen showed initial interest in the product. In most of these situations, the Arabian businessmen were being polite by not directly rejecting the business advances, or they were trying to get rid of the pressure sales tactics.

Decisions are made in slow and cautious steps. So you need patience, a good character that exhibits honesty, trustworthiness, and willingness to develop a human relationship before a business one. To close a deal expect to have many meetings (sometimes up to 6 meetings in a period of 2 weeks).

To help understand your Arabian clients, the following are some signs that your client is very interested in your business:

- They ask to meet with you more than once.
- They are putting a lot of effort into the negotiation process.
- After hearing your offer, they inform you of their company success stories, the amount of business they do, and the benefits of granting them your business and product distribution rights.

After The Meeting

Slow business beginnings

Business in the Arabian region has a relaxed atmosphere and moves slowly; you need to be patient in order to see the results of your efforts. The slow pace of business beginnings in some cases can also be attributed to government bureaucracies and set procedures.

In Kuwait, for example, if you intend to sell oil tools, medical devices, or army and police equipment, you must go through certain procedures. First, you have to locate a Kuwaiti company to act as your exclusive agent. Your chosen business partner has to register the agency with the Ministry of Commerce. Samples and catalogs of the product will be provided to a number of government bodies assigned to test and study the product. When the government specifies its needs, they will use their list of Kuwaiti agents and the products they represent to place their offers. Because of that, sometimes it will take 6 to 12 months for your Kuwaiti agent to place the first purchase order.

Arabian companies weaknesses

A considerable number of Arabian companies lack marketing skills and experience in customer support. You can improve this situation by providing your distributors and agents with an Arabic translation of your product literature and catalogs. You can also set up a regular training schedule to enhance their marketing and customer service skills. To ensure that your agents and distributors are not attaching negative experiences to your product name, suggest to them a set of procedures and steps to follow in handling complaints, returns, and the like. Do not just provide them with a copy of the procedures you are using in your country. Ask for assistance and feedback from your new agents to ensure that the plans accommodate the different environment.

A friend of mine who is the president of a medical company in the USA complained to me of his distributor in Saudi Arabia. The Saudi distributor had cut down on the quantity and the frequency of his orders. I promised my friend to check his Saudi distributor during my next trip to the Middle East. My investigation showed that the Saudi distributor did not have an adequate distribution network outside his local zone in Saudi Arabia. At the beginning, the Saudi distributor invested a good effort to introduce the product to different regions in Saudi Arabia and because the product itself was unique, orders were coming from all parts of the market. However, the distributor did not upgrade his distribution capabilities to accommodate the expansion of his client base. The orders kept coming, but the delivery was either late or nonexistent. With time, the Saudi distributor was avoided by many of his out of area new clients and the end consumer trust in the product itself was negatively affected. As a solution to the problem, two options were valid. One was to locate another distributor with a stronger and wider distribution network. The other option was to have more than one distributor, each covering their territory.

Joint efforts

I observed that most successful imported products in the Arabian region have behind them good communication and joint efforts in marketing and customer support between the agent or distributor and the foreign manufacturer of the product. As a manufacturer or a service provider, if you do your homework at the beginning stage of searching for representatives, you will save yourself a lot of headaches, lost efforts, and negative or weak product appearance in the new market. If you are financially capable of visiting your potential distributors or agents, you should do it. This way you can experience and observe the market, check your potential agent's distribution network, and the level of management, marketing, and customer support they provide.

The joint efforts you and your agent will put forward for the product will profit both of your businesses. A product with a good support, marketing, distribution, and reputation will easily be the leader of the pack. The more you are involved in establishing your product in the new market, the more experience and valuable information you will gain and the better relationship you will have with your distributors.

Agreements

To ensure that any problems that might arise between you and your agent can be solved and to guarantee that your agent will be a source of information, I advise you to add to the agency or distribution contract any special clauses, terms, and conditions which give you the right to be involved in marketing and customer support and the right to perform inspection visits when needed. You can also request a regular feedback report from your agent with information about current problems, competitive products comparison, suggestions, etc.

Handling quote requests

Expect that your clients will request that you give them a lower price or extend a discount citing many reasons for the request:
- It is their first order.
- They have received a better pricing from another overseas supplier.
- They can obtain the same items locally for the same cost you quoted them or even a little bit higher than what you quoted them. In this case they prefer the local supplier even if it cost them a little bit more because they take into account delivery time and the amount of time and effort it will take to obtain it from an overseas source.

- The quoted price (after adding to it shipping and tariff costs) will not enable them to sell it locally with a good profit margin or they will not be able to compete with other similar products in the market.
- This initial order is just to test the acceptance it will have in their local market (especially if the product is new to the market). Because of that they believe it is a risky/uncertain situation and thus would like to have the overseas supplier to encourage such test by offering a better price.

Price negotiation is part of doing business in the Arabian market. It is considered an art and a way to enjoy doing business (or the business game). Once given the previously listed reasons or some other ones, it is important to know that it is not always the case that they are only trying to get a better pricing from you but it could be a valid reason and an accurate description of the current situation.

Other strategies your Arab clients might use to get a better pricing from you could be:

- Their initial quotation request does not specify a quantity but implies that the quantity will depend on the pricing you will provide them with, which might lead you to think that the better pricing you provide, the more quantities they will be requesting. This might not always be valid. Sometimes, after they have received your quote, they will place a small order (which may have been decided before they placed their initial request with you).

- They might place a quote request for a huge quantity which will probably cause you to give them the best price you have. After that you might receive their order for a smaller quantity but for the same quoted unit price you provided in the first place. Now they know what your bottom price is and will start negotiating from that point.

What to do in such cases:
- Do not lose your coolness or express any emotions of mistrust or anger. Remember that this is part of doing business and a fun thing to do.
- When you receive a quotation request without specifying a quantity or a quotation request with a huge quantity, don't rush to give your best and bottom pricing. Expect that price negotiations will follow and you want to be able to make more profit for your company and at the same time be able to give your Arabian client discount so he can know you are flexible with him and that he have achieved a better price for his company when he negotiated with you.
- Before providing a quote, if possible, do some research to know the pricing of the same product or similar ones in the destination market.
- It is a good idea in every quote you give, to provide them with a quantity/price quote. Which means your quote specifies certain prices for a range of quantities. In this way, in future correspondences, you have a range to work with instead of negotiating on the bottom price you have offered.

Handling Letters Of Credit

Some Arabian companies prefer to pay using a letter of credit especially when it is one of the first business purchases from a new foreign supplier. An irrevocable confirmed letter of credit is a secure payment method for both, the buyer and the seller. There also might be another reason for using a letter of credit on the part of your Arabian partner. When the Arabian company has won a tender in which the government is the final destination or the end user for the goods, then the Arabian company will not receive its money from the government until the goods have been delivered and sometimes it takes from one to two months to receive the payment. In this scenario, some Arabian companies prefer to use their banks in handling payments for these purchases.

As a US supplier, you might encounter some difficulties in finding a US bank that will be willing to accept and honor the letter of credit you will receive. You will face a bigger challenge in finding a US bank that can provide you with a back to back letter of credit that is secured on the basis of the original letter of credit you receive from your Arabian client.

Exporters might need a back to back letter of credit in the case that they don't have enough financial resources to purchase the goods or they prefer to use this method when it is available to them because it will not tie any of their money to a specific export operation. From my experience I found that using US-Arabian banks will greatly facilitate handling letters of credits. For a list of these banks refer to appendix D.

Advertising & Marketing

It is very helpful to provide your clients with literature that is produced in their own language, especially if the literature will be passed by your overseas partners to their customers. You can solicit the help of your overseas local agent when producing such materials or ask him to recommend to you a local advertising/translation agency to handle the job. If you intend on using a local translation service provider (i.e. a company residing in your area), be sure that they fully understand the targeted language, audience and market. Producing a word by word translation of your current local product literature will not necessarily prove to be an effective equivalent of the original and in some cases might yield the opposite of your intended message. Every market has its own marketing and advertising rules and every audience is approached differently. I am sure that you have heard about some companies resulting to changing the name of their products when introduced to a foreign market because an exact translation proved to be ineffective or in some cases offensive.

Advertisement produced for the Arabian countries should avoid using sexual appeal or sexual innuendoes in its message. It should be conservative in content and appearance and does not present any social values or situations that contradict with the Arabian culture or Islam. In almost all the Arabian countries advertisement should not directly or explicitly contain comparison between two different brands for the same type of products. Message should place more emphasis on the quality and functionality of the product. The main advertisement outlet sources are newspapers, magazines and television. Telemarketing and mail-marketing are nonexistent. Telemarketing goes against the Arabian culture because it is viewed as an invasion of privacy and a bad excuse to place a call (to say the least). In recent years, the use of professional Arabian advertising agencies has been increasing although the industry still lacks in clear guidelines and regulations. More Arabian businesses are realizing the importance of advertising but the majority still views it as an accessory not a necessity.

How to Win Your Arab Clients' Friendship & Business

The following suggestions to deepen your relationship and business with your Arabian clients might also be valid when dealing with any foreign culture. The more you know about your clients and their customers, the more accurate and adequate your decisions and business policies will be.

- Learn about the culture of your clients as much as possible. Try to know what is appreciated and what is disliked in their culture in terms of habits, traditions, and business interactions, and utilize that knowledge.

- Study the environment that surrounds your clients' businesses in terms of laws, regulations, difficulties, opportunities, and the like.

- Develop more than a business relationship and seek your clients' friendship by showing a genuine interest in their culture, being flexible, serving their other needs, and maintaining a continuous communication channel regardless of business activities and volume. I always let my clients know that I will be glad and honored to help them with any needs. For example, I would help them get information about a US vacation destination or information about a US university. Keeping the communication channel open can be as simple as frequently sending a thank you or congratulations or postcards which say we appreciate your friendship and business.

- Be patient, always ask for their feedback, invite them to share their opinions and suggestions in the decisions and policies that involve them, listen attentively and try to understand what they are communicating to you without underestimating their knowledge or overestimating yours. Remember that it is their market that both of you are discussing.

- When you offer your products and services to new overseas clients, you will notice that some will respond to you immediately while many will not. That is especially true when dealing with the Arabian market. Some of the companies you contact have an immediate need or in the near future need and that's why they correspond with you very fast. So what are going to decide about the companies that did not respond to your offer of cooperation? Amazingly enough, I noticed that many companies in this situation will simply drop these contacts from their list. The question is, what happened to the art of marketing? The basic element in an effective marketing plan is consistency and repetition. When you continue to remind these companies of you and your products and services through continuously providing them with the latest catalogs, new releases, your business newsletter, and the like, you are actually building recognition with them for your business and establishing a trust in you through the repetition of your correspondences even if it was a one way communication process. This is the same method you use to get your local customers to recognize your company. The same applies to overseas clients. As you normally expect that a new product needs a marketing plan to draw local consumers, with new overseas clients you also need a marketing plan. Arabian businesses are cautious and take their time when approached by a new overseas company. They need to develop a trust relationship with the foreign supplier. Recognition is a step to achieving that, so do not give up too soon.

Employ the following in your business:

- Flexibility in payment terms.

- Regular visits to your agents to better understand the market and build more than a business relationship. If your company is financially capable, you can greatly benefit by transferring one of your international representatives to your foreign agent's company.

- Provide financial and professional support to your agents in the field of marketing, such as advertisements, seminars, training, etc.

Remember that you are actually investing in your product's marketing and sales.

- Employ enough centralization and authority in your export or international sales department in order to increase the speed of your response and delivery to your agents and clients inquiries and orders.

- Set your international prices competitively by studying comparable products in the targeted market.

Chapter 4

Cultural Customs & Social Structure

This section of the book contains information about Arab customs followed in social interactions, eating and drinking, invitations, dressing, and other daily activities. Notice that these customs are the general rules in the Arab region, but every Arabian country has its own variations of these general customs.

Conservative behavior

In public, Arabs behave conservatively. Display of affection between spouses is nonexistent. It is a private society and display of one's feelings is kept private. You will also notice that laughter and joking in public is toned down, which is not the case in private gatherings. Arguments between spouses, friends, and people in general are also kept private or conducted in a way that guarantees no one else is aware of it.

Privacy

Because of the importance of privacy in the Arabian society, houses are built with big solid walls that maintain privacy from street traffic and the neighbors. One of the most important considerations in building a house is the guarantee that the residents of the house can't see their neighbors from any part of the house, thus insuring the privacy of the neighbors. When I visit the house of an Arabian relative or friend, the standing position I will take next to the house door should insure that when the door is open I can't see the inside of the house. Furthermore, I will not go inside until my host signals me to do so by extending his right hand with his palm up saying "Tafaddal", which means "come in".

What is a Dewaniah?

In every Arabian house, especially in the GCC region, there is a room called "Dewaniah" or "Majless" for guests' gatherings. Most of these Dewaniahs are for male visitors only. The Dewaniah is usually located close to the outside main entrance, away from the rest of the house. Women guests gather in a room inside the house and sometimes get to their gathering room from an outside entrance specifically assigned for female visitors. In some parts of the Arabian region men and women who are not directly blood related to each other or not married to each other don't mix. That's why there are often separate guest gathering rooms for both genders in the same house. In some Arabian houses this rule of gender separation is not followed.

Some Dewaniahs open on a daily basis and others once weekly. This regular gathering is a chance for relatives, friends, and invited guests to check on each other and converse in many subjects. It is a form of socializing where people communicate the latest news about other relatives, economy, business, sports, politics, etc. Tea, coffee, and sometimes a light snack are served.

When invited to a Dewaniah

If you are invited to a Dewaniah, you are not expected to bring food, drinks, or gifts. Muslims pray 5 times daily where each prayer lasts for about 15 minutes: at dawn, midday, mid-afternoon, sunset, and nightfall. Prayers are usually held at the Islamic worship places called "Mosques". Regular gathering in Dewaniahs usually takes place after nightfall prayer and sometimes between the sunset and the nightfall prayers.

Upon entering the house as you approach the Dewaniah notice the Dewaniah's door. If shoes and sandals were left at the door by other guests, then take off your shoes. It is customary when entering a Dewaniah or an office to greet everyone there by saying "Alsalamo-Alikom", which means "peace be with you" and it is the equivalent of saying "hello". The reply to this greeting is "Wa'alikom Alsalam". Once inside the Dewaniah, everyone will stand up to greet you and shake your hand. Start with the person standing on your right side or the one who is approaching you. If you are a first time visitor or elderly, most likely your host and the attendants will offer you a seat at the head of the Dewaniah as a sign of respect and honor.

Some Dewaniahs are furnished with couches; traditional ones don't have couches and attendants sit on the floor. The floor is covered with Persian rugs and against the walls of the Dewaniah there are pillows to rest your back against. Notice that in both modern and traditional Dewaniahs, attendants are seated in a circle to ensure that no one is facing someone else's back. Also, remember the rule that the soles of your feet should not point directly toward someone else.

In office or Dewaniah visits you might be offered Arabian coffee, which is served in small cups without sugar or milk. The coffee server will keep filling up your cup until you signal that you are done by slightly shaking your empty cup and either saying "Bass, Shokrann", which means "no more, thank you", or by covering the cup with the palm of your hand while returning the cup to the coffee server.

Remember that you should always use your right hand. It is strongly advisable that you accept at least one cup of coffee as a way of honoring this traditional hospitality.

Greeting women

When you are visiting your Arabian host's office or home and you are introduced to a female worker or a female relative of your host, in all cases you should not greet her with a kiss. If the woman extends her hand to greet you, you may shake her hand; otherwise greeting with words only is appropriate.

Admiring objects and gift giving

When you explicitly admire a possession of your Arabian host, he might feel obligated to offer it to you even if it is of special value to him. Admiring something should not be prolonged.

When Arabs receive gifts, it is a custom not to open it in front of the giver. The same is expected when they give someone else a gift.

Pampering guests

The Arabian culture stresses the importance of honoring guests and pampering them. The host will try his best to insure that his guests are very comfortable. The host will serve food in excessive quantities to insure that every guest will be fully satisfied. Another custom is that the host and his sons should be the last ones to start eating as a sign of honoring the guests. Also, even if the host has actually finished eating, he will continue to act as if he is still eating until everyone else has finished. In this way, the host insures that the guests were not rushed into finishing.

If you are invited to dinner or lunch in a restaurant, it is customary that your Arabian host pay for it. It will leave a nice effect on your Arabian guest if you do the same when he visits you. When you invite your Arabian partners, note that Muslims are forbidden by the religion from consuming alcohol or eating pork products.

Invitation to Join & Share

Another Arabian cultural habit is invitation to join and share. If someone visits or drop by a friend (or even happen to be passing by someone they don't know) and food was present, an invitation to join and share the food will be sincerely extended. It is considered rude not to place an invitation. Of course you can decline after thanking them for their generosity.

"Save Face" concept

The Arabian culture is a non-confrontational one which seeks the least conflict possible. A concept called "save face" is a way to solve conflicts and avoid embarrassing or discomforting the parties involved. Saving someone's face or dignity involves using maneuvers or holding one's reactions to give the other party a way to exit the situation with minimal discomfort or harm to their dignity. It involves compromise, patience, and sometimes looking the other way to allow things time to get back to normal. The "save face" concept is looked at as a behavior of high quality ethics and manners. The Arabian culture encourages people to act humbly and with sensitivity to a person's dignity, especially when that person's dignity and self respect is endangered.

This concept of sensitivity is not limited to extreme situations only. For example, when someone is pressuring an Arabian businessman into committing himself to a matter that is not of interest or beyond his capability, he might indirectly refuse the matter by offering to study the subject, which might be interpreted as a yes answer. So, remember no pressure sales tactics because they cause discomfort and might associate you as a person with unpleasant presence. There is no separation between you as a person and the business you represent or conduct in the Arabian world. Business is not only business.

Men's clothing

The majority of men in the GCC region wear a long sleeved one piece dress that covers the whole body, called a "Dishdashah" or "Thoub". This garment allows the air to circulate, which helps cool the body during the hot summer days. During summer, the Dishdashah is usually made of white cotton to reflect sunlight. In winter, the Dishdashah is made from heavier fabric such as wool and comes in darker colors. With the Dishdashah men also wear a 3-piece head cover. The bottom piece of this head covering is a white cap that is sometimes filled with holes. This cap, called "Thagiyah", is used to hold the hair in place. On top of the Thagiyah is a scarf-like head cover that comes in two types: a light, white head cover called "Gutrah" which is worn in summer, and a heavy red and white checked head cover called "Shumag" which is worn during winter.

These head covers protect the head from direct sunlight and can be used to cover the mouth and the nose during sand storms or cold weather. On top of the Thagiyah and the Gutrah is the "Ogal", which is a black band surrounding the top of the head to hold everything else in place. When male children reach puberty they are taught to wear the head covering as a sign for entering manhood. Inside the house, the head covering is not needed; when someone has guests in his house he wears it as a sign of respect.

Women's clothing

The majority of Arabian women dress conservatively. Some women dress in clothes that do not cover their faces or hair, while others cover them. For example, a very conservative woman might wear a long black garment called "Abayah" that covers her body from the shoulders down to her feet. Under this cover she could be wearing a traditional Arabian dress in full body length with long sleeves and filled with beautiful bead work, or she could be wearing the latest style from an internationally known designer.

In addition to the Abayah, a very conservative woman would also wear a face and head cover. Some women would wear the Abayah without the head and face cover, while others might wear a scarf-like cover called "Hejab" that covers the hair but not the face.

Family structure

In an Arabian family, gender and age plays a big role in specifying responsibilities. The father is usually the head of the family and the provider for its needs, while the mother plays a major role in raising children and taking care of the house. This structure is not always the norm; in recent years, both the father and the mother provide for family needs, while household chores are taken care of by foreign maids and servants. In the past, most major family decisions were made by the father, but recently some of these decisions are made jointly by both the father and the mother.

Sons and daughters are taught to follow the inherited traditions and are given responsibilities that correspond with their age and gender. Sons are usually taught to be protectors of their sisters and to help the father with his duties inside and outside the house, while daughters are taught to be the source of love and emotional support in the family, as well as helping their mother to take care of household chores.

Winds of change do not spare any culture; the changes that entered the structure of some Arabian houses is not due to economical needs, but education for both men and women that is mandated by law in the Arabian countries. Education from kindergarten up to university degrees is free to nationals and sometimes residents of these Arabian countries.

Although culture, traditions, and Islam strongly stress the importance of women's roles in taking care of the house and raising children, it is a mistake to think that Arabian women are confined to this role. Before Islam there were many successful Arabian businesswomen and they still exist throughout the Arabian region, but because of cultural reasons, they conduct business in an inconspicuous way.

Families with lots of sons and daughters still exist, but in recent years the average size of the family has decreased. A daughter lives at her family house as long as she is not married; once she is married she moves to her husband's home. Sons might move to their own houses when they get married, but at least one son will still live at the family house even if he is married in order to take care of the parents. When a woman gets married there are no changes made to any part of her name.

Social duties

Society members perform a number of customary social duties. When someone comes back from a trip, his relatives, friends, and neighbors will drop by to greet him.

The same happens when someone is ill and confined to his home or staying in a hospital. Everyone will visit him to give moral support, check on him, and keep him company to ease his stay. When visiting an ill person, visitors will usually bring food, chocolate, or fruits, and occasionally flowers. Even when someone is ill and staying at the hospital, his sons, closest relatives, or friends will show hospitality to visitors by serving them refreshments or coffee and chocolate.

When two people get married, their relatives, friends, and neighbors will bring gifts, which are usually either money or something that is useful for the newly- established home. When a woman has a new baby, her relatives, friends, and neighbors visit her to congratulate her and to present her with gifts. The father of the new baby is also visited by his relatives, friends, and neighbors to congratulate him. The mother of the new baby will usually spend the first 40 days after the delivery in her family house, where she will be taken care of by her mother and sisters.

The Arab culture is detail oriented. Ethics and expected social behaviors, like generosity, respect, and caring, are not only definitions but are translated into customs and social duties. On all the occasions I have listed in the previous paragraph, there are customary sentences to be said which correspond with the occasion. The following are some of the customary sayings, the occasion, and the translated meaning:

- When visiting an ill person: "Maa Teshoof Sharr, Ajer Waafia en Shaa Allah": I pray that you don't see harm, and by Allah's (god) will, you will be rewarded for your patience and suffering and you will be cured.
- When visiting someone who returned from a trip: "Al Hamdo Lillah Ala Al Salamah": I thank god for bringing you back safe.
- When visiting someone who has a new baby: "Yetrabba Be Ezzekum, Waa Allah Yajaluhoh Min El Thorriah Al Salehah": May he/she (the new baby) be raised in your goodness and may god make him/her be a good son/daughter.
- When visiting someone who is getting married; "Mabrook": Congratulations.

Chapter 5
Cultural Customs & Social Structure

No matter what method you choose to locate your overseas clients, you have to first familiarize yourself with the targeted market. Try to obtain as much data as possible about the political climate, business regulations, current needs, business culture, etc. This information can be captured by getting in touch with business people that are exporting to your targeted market, especially the ones that sell a different product than yours, so they would not view you as a possible competitor. Another way to acquire information is through communicating with US cultural associations or attending cultural gatherings that represent the targeted region.

In the second section of this chapter, I have included other ways to obtain market information and to get connected. To ensure maximum and successful utilization of the connections you will have, you should first study the market, know the guidelines, devise a plan, and then approach the market.

What to Look For

Because of the strong and lasting family, friends, and tribal connections in the Arabian world, you will notice that almost everyone knows everyone else. The stronger the tie, the more favoritism is evident in business management positions and business transactions. Companies generally represent the owner's family. The owner, his immediate family members, and relatives occupy the high management and decision-making positions.

Who should represent your business?

If you intend to sell oil tools, medical devices, or army and police equipment, government ministries will be the biggest buyers of your products or services. Choosing a company that is experienced in and extensively participating in government tenders is an important factor. The more involvement and experience a company has with government projects and tenders, the more business it will bring to you. These companies are closer to sources of information and therefore have first hand and comprehensive knowledge of current needs and upcoming projects in the country.

If your target market is consumers, you should look for representatives that have experience selling similar products, or companies that are ready to employ an experienced staff to handle your product. It is also important not to rule out new or less-experienced companies. Younger companies are eager to do business and might have more interest and enthusiasm in marketing your product.

Many Arabian companies are involved in diverse fields simultaneously. It is not unusual to find a company that successfully sells medical equipment, computers, and food products at the same time.

Be aware

One of the complaints I have heard many times from American companies who have a distributor or an agent in the Arabian market is that their representative is doing nothing to sell their products, or his sales of their products have gone down to zero after some time. In some cases, this is due to the fact that some Arabian companies put out a great effort to obtain the agency or distribution rights. Once they have this right, their efforts in marketing and selling the product are nonexistent. These companies either lack marketing skills, or their attention is turned to obtaining the agency of another product. Some companies like to collect as many agencies as they can in the hope that the products will market themselves. The main source for their continuation and profit in the market is some old agencies they had when the market was not so competitive. To avoid being in this situation, ask for a list of companies they represent; communicate with the most recent companies on the list and get their feedback.

A fear Arabian companies have when representing a foreign business is that their efforts in marketing and selling the product might be harvested by another Arabian company when the first agency expires. Your agent might not be inclined to spend money and energy promoting your product if he fears that another company may take over the agency.

The conditions of the agency or distribution agreement between you and your Arabian partner might determine the success or failure of your agent's marketing efforts. If the agreement simply states that the agency rights given to the Arabian company expire after one year and performance evaluations will be the deciding factor in extending it for another year, the Arabian agent might feel uncertain about the advisability of dedicating his money and time to this product because of the possibility of losing the agency in the second year.

If the contract clearly states reasonable sales goals that will be considered a sign of success in this partnership, and used as the binding condition in continuing this agreement, then both the foreign business and the agent have protected their rights and can proceed with their functions without unnecessary worries.

How to Locate US & Overseas Business Partners & Obtain Market Information

There are several ways that companies can locate agents overseas. These include traveling to countries of interest, using an international trading company, initiating communication using a list that was purchased from an international leads provider, or using databases that are provided free of charge by various USA government offices.

Foreign students

Another method, which is frequently overlooked, is through communicating with foreign students. In 1989, *while I was a student at California State University, an American friend of mine told me that a friend of his father grew pistachios and various nuts and that he was interested in exporting his products to Kuwait. I met with the American producer and answered questions regarding the Kuwaiti market's consumption of pistachios and nuts. Arabs serve these products with tea almost every day and they are heavily used in making desserts. The American producer asked me if I could connect him to a Kuwaiti distributor, which I did.*

This move on the part of this American business did not cost them anything. They had their foreign market information and connection in just one meeting. There are a lot of foreign students studying international trading or business in universities all over the United States and within any country. Your company can contact students from the countries you are interested in. Even if they can't get you connected, at least they are a valuable information source for your targeted foreign market.

Obtaining leads lists & using exporters

Using leads lists provided by an international information provider or government databases has its drawbacks. The leads and market information are usually out of date and very limited, but sometimes do get you to communicate successfully with an overseas company. International trading companies, like exporters, can help you in selling your products internationally by acting as your agent. Unless you are using an excellent and experienced exporter, the drawback in this service is that you are not communicating with your foreign market directly, which means valuable information is not reaching you. Also, in some cases your product marketing, customer support, and reputation are completely controlled by and dependent on the exporter himself.

Some exporters provide a service for a commission and/or a fee, in which they act as your agent in the search for a foreign distributor. When the foreign partner is located, the exporter's role ends and you can communicate directly with your new foreign partner.

Visiting the foreign market

If your company is financially capable, you can send your international sales people on overseas business trips. Meeting face to face with different companies helps you to make an educated choice of who should represent your business. While visiting these companies, you can observe their work place, employees, and management. At the same time, you can check their distribution network, marketing plans, customer support level, and how well the other products they represent are doing in the market. You may also have the opportunity to study other competitive products and obtain very useful information.

On-line networks

One of the latest powerful channels to trade internationally is through on-line network, like the Internet. By joining an international trading forum, you will have access to very useful information about markets and opportunities all over the world. You will be able to communicate with other traders in almost every country in the world.

Advertising in US magazines

Advertising about your company in internationally distributed magazines (like the ones available on airplanes) can draw international attention to your products. There are a number of USA magazines that specialize in the arena of international trading, providing good insight into current opportunities and market research. One time I advertised in one of these magazines about a service my company provides. Most of the early responses I received were from the USA but shortly after, requests for our service came from Australia, China, Thailand, United Arab Emirates, and many other countries. See Appendix A for a list of US international trade magazines.

Advertising in Arabian newspapers & magazines

There are a number of Arabian newspapers and magazines (English edition) distributed in the United States. These publications provide more specialized and current information about the Arabian region. You can advertise in their other publications that are distributed in the Arabian world. A list containing some of the Arabian newspapers and magazines is provided in Appendix B.

US Department Of Commerce- Desk Officers

For every country, there is a Country Desk Officer at the US Department Of Commerce, International Trade Administration. At every information desk, there is a person knowledgeable in business related to his countries of specialization. This is a source for free useful information. Some of what they can help with:

- Commercial payment disputes
- Agreements
- Statistics
- Information about a particular trade sector
- Information about franchising
- Best prospects for USA companies
- Setting appointments with foreign companies
- Information about joint ventures

For information regarding Arabian countries you can contact the desk officers at the office of the Near East at the International Trade Administration. For more information refer to Appendix E.

The office of the Near East provides a fax on demand system called Flash Facts. Flash Facts provides a huge selection of general and country specific documents that you can select from. The system will fax the chosen documents to the fax number you specify. You can start be requesting document number 0100 which contains a list of currently available documents. You can access the very friendly and easy to use Flash Facts system by dialing (202) 482-1064.

National Trade Data Bank

Many USA embassies around the world produce monthly reports pertaining to the country they are located in. These reports include information about new laws, market research, upcoming projects, exhibits, key business contacts, and companies looking for US products. The reports are provided in a government database known as the National Trade Data Bank or the NTDB. The NTDB, which is a big and comprehensive trade information source, consists of over 130 databases.

The following is a listing for some of the subjects covered in the NTDB:

- Basic export information
- Guides to doing business in foreign countries
- International trade regulations
- Country reports
- Calendars of trade shows and exhibitions
- Trade leads
- Market reports
- Export regulations
- Export and import statistics
- Export yellow pages
- SBA news and loan programs
- US foreign trade highlights
- World FactBook
- American chambers of commerce abroad
- Small business guide to exporting
- Country commercial guides

The NTDB is updated on a monthly basis and can be accessed through the Internet for a small subscription fee. You can also purchase the monthly CD-ROM version or access it free of charge at most Department Of Commerce district offices or through federal depository libraries. Refer to Appendix F for more details.

The Export Yellow Pages

This is one way to get your company name marketed worldwide and for free. The Export Yellow Pages is a database of US suppliers that are interested in exporting. The hard copy of this database can be obtained for free by contacting your local US Department Of Commerce District Office. The database can also be found in the National Trade Data Bank. This directory is published once a year and distributed to US embassies around the world. Foreign companies regularly check with US embassies in their countries to identify possible US business partners. You can list your company in the Export Yellow Pages free of charge by requesting the registration form your local US Department Of Commerce District Office (see Appendix M).

Foreign Chambers Of Commerce

You can provide foreign chambers of commerce with your company information and your products catalog. The information you provide will be available to the chambers members and to other businesses looking for certain products. Some of these chambers produce a monthly magazine that might showcase your products. All of that is for free (of course you pick up the overseas mailing costs). For a list of Arabian chambers of commerce please refer to appendix K. For a more extensive reference, you can purchase the "World Chamber Of Commerce Directory" which is published annually. This directory contains a listing for US chambers of commerce, foreign chambers of commerce in the US, foreign chambers of commerce throughout the world, US embassies, foreign embassies in the US, foreign tourist information bureaus, and more. For more information on this directory, please refer to appendix L.

International trade associations

There are a number of US international trade and export associations. These associations include experienced international traders covering every spot in the world. Joining them can help to increase your business internationally and provide you with valuable data about your primary market and other opportunities around the world. Many businesses started their international move with resources available in these associations. The benefits of being a member are extensive and valuable to your business:

- Valuable source for information, experiences and connections
- Monthly meetings where guest speakers are experienced world traders from various fields and interests

- Effective resource for networking with other exporters and service providers.
- Some associations regularly have foreign visiting delegations, which is a great chance to get connected overseas.
- Many associations provide a members directory that will be available to other related businesses, visiting delegations, and international entities in the US. The directories market your name and bring business to your company
- Being a member gives your business more credibility in the eyes of national and international clients

Other associations

Joining associations related to your service or industry (other than international trading associations) may increase your international dealings. Many associations have foreign members, and many foreign companies contact these associations looking for business partners. For a list of international trade and other associations, check your public library and appendix I.

Arabian trade shows & exhibits

Participating in trade shows and exhibits held in your targeted foreign market are a direct and very effective method to establish connections. Various Arabian exhibit organizers are listed in Appendix C. Contact these companies to obtain information about the exhibits they organize. You can also contact Arabian embassies in the United States and ask them to provide a list of future trade shows. Embassies can also assist you with questions regarding visa requirements, export documentation, and current regulations

US trade shows & exhibits

Big trade shows and exhibits in the US are frequently attended by foreign companies looking for products to purchase or represent. Pick the trade shows you should participate in by studying their attendance statistics. You can find references for US trade shows and exhibits in your public library.

Business directories

Every international trader knows the importance of being able to locate suppliers and buyers. There are many printed directories that can be used to achieve that, but if you want to speed this process, save your time and effort, and truly maximize your efficiency, you should look into business directories that are stored on CD-ROM's.

Depending on the CD-ROM you choose, you will be able to search for suppliers and prospective buyers in an easy and fast way. Most directories on the market today give the choice of searching for your targeted companies by specifying their SIC code (Standard Industrial Classification), their geographical location, their Zip code, and other criteria.

The following are some of the CD-ROM's you can find on the market. Some of these CD-ROM's cover the US market while others cover other markets. Depending on what country your business is located in, some of these directories will give you connections to a foreign market while others will connect you to your local market.

Kompass Directories (on CD-ROM and Printed form), published by Kompass. Business directories covering more than 30 countries. Contains detailed information about thousands of companies and their products, services, and contact information. Countries covered include Australia, Belgium, China, France, Germany, India, Korea, Saudi Arabia, Spain, Sweden, United Arab Emirates, United Kingdom, USA, and other countries.

Business America On CD-ROM, published by American Business Information Inc. Contains a listing of more than 10 million USA businesses. You can search by SIC code, number of employees, professional specialty, geographic area, and company name. Every record includes company name, address, telephone number, key contact name and title, SIC code, credit rating code, number of employees, and annual sales volume. Available on annual lease basis.

PhoneDisc Business, published by Digital Directory Assistance Inc. Contains 10 million US businesses. You can search by name, address, phone number, SIC code, and SIC description. Search can be limited by city, state, street, zip code, area code, and companies containing a specific word within their name. Other features include a counter for search results, dialing a selected company, exporting search results to a file in many different formats, and printing search results as a list or as different formats of address labels. There is no limit on mailing or exporting business listings.

Directory Of US Importers & Directory Of US Exporters, published by the Journal Of Commerce. Provided in a printed form, on diskette, and on CD-ROM. These directories contain detailed information on thousands of US importers/exporters. It provides full contact information, import/export country, port, commodities, SIC codes, banks, number of employees, and other data. These directories are not only useful to locate your possible business export or import partner, but you can also use them to know who your competitors are and what are the values and numbers of their shipments.

For a list of other CD-ROM's containing business directories and market information, you can purchase the current edition of CD-ROM Pocket Guide from bookstores or contact the publishers at 203-761-1466.

For more information on the directories previously mentioned, please refer to Appendix H.

Chapter 6
Choosing Your
International Staff

Why is it important?

Choosing the right international staff is an important factor in your company's success in the international market. I have witnessed many deals, opportunities, company's reputations, and efforts go down the drain because of the unprofessional behavior and ignorance of its international sales and marketing people. Having set criteria for choosing your international staff will speed your work and save your money, efforts, and reputation.

Basic information

The following is an example of how ignorance in basic information could make you lose business and reveal your weak understanding about the foreign market.

An American manufacturer was selling his *products to a Kuwaiti company without an agency or a distribution agreement between them, just a basic export-import relationship. Another Kuwaiti company contacted the manufacturer with the intention of representing them in Kuwait as their exclusive agent. The American manufacturer's export manager responded by suggesting that they share the exclusive agency with the first Kuwaiti company. His idea was that each company would cover the area in which it was located. The export manager did not spend a few seconds looking at a map of Kuwait. If he did,he would have discovered that Kuwait is a small country and one agent is more than enough. Even if Kuwait was a big country, if he had done simple research he would have discovered that the distance between these two Kuwaiti companies was less than a mile! The American manufacturer lost the business of both Kuwaiti companies.*

Seizing opportunities

Your international team should be able and willing to investigate opportunities that knock on its door. Some of these opportunities are genuine and worth looking into.

A number of Arabian companies complained to me *that they had not received answers to their offers of cooperation with some US companies. To my surprise, when I initiated the requests with the US companies on behalf of the Arabian companies, I discovered that most of these US businesses were interested in such offers; the rest did not respond because they already had agents in those countries. Why didn't the interested US companies respond to direct requests from these Arabian businesses? In rare cases some of the letters or fax messages sent by the Arabian companies were misplaced or lost. Most often though, the reason was pure negligence and the inability to recognize what these messages represented. One reason given by an international sales representative was that parts of the fax message he received were not clear. Another export sales manager explained that the quotation request he had received was not detailed enough! In these cases, the solution is simply to spend* one minute to respond to these

Arabian companies with one line only "Please send more details" or "Please re-fax your message".

Basic communication skills

One day A USA manufacturer contacted my *company wanting a connection to the Middle East market. He knew about my business from an advertisement in a US international trading magazine. The products the manufacturer wanted to export were very salable in the Middle East. My company responded that his products would have a good response from the companies that we would approach. We offered to market his products and connect him to his new distributors all over the Middle East, under the condition of signing our standard Finder's Agreement. He objected to one of the conditions we had in our proposed Finder's Agreement. He asked us to waive our onetime fee. The fee is fully refundable by the end of the Finder's Agreement if we were not able to connect his company to the Middle East market. We explained to him that the philosophy behind the fee is to cover a small percentage of the costs we will incur in marketing, research, and communication and to guarantee the seriousness and dedication of the subscribers to this time and money consuming operation. Objecting to any condition in the agreement is part of negotiating but the reasons behind the objection should be presented in a professional and intelligent way. In a fax message he listed a couple of export companies that he had used before, but these companies were not up to the job and he had lost around $300 in purchasing leads from them. His words were "What if your*

*service turns out to be like the other two companies ......
From our previous experiences, we don't place big trust in
middlemen promises".*

*First of all, we did not offer to sell him leads, we offered
to do the job ourselves. Second, we provided him with
references of US and other companies who have used our
service before. He could have checked with them if he was
worried about our service. Third, he could have suggested
waiving the fee or adding a condition to it without insulting
us. Our reply to him was to reject his offer and
communication was discontinued.*

I have found that impressions shown in the initial
communication stage with a company is often an indication
of how well the partnership will perform. Be sure that your
international staff knows basic communication skills.
Customer service skills of making clients feel respected,
appreciated, and listened to should also be practiced in other
departments in the company.

I am sure that you have encountered a company
employee with a poor attitude, un-professional behavior, or
lack of communication skills that drove your business away.
This employee, without any doubt, is costing his company
considerably more than his salary only. Imagine having him
or her as your international representative or export
manager, dealing with people of different cultures and the
need to be patient, sensitive, and welcoming.

Your international sales people should be open minded,
prompt, willing to expand some effort to understand the

culture of their clients, patient, able to evaluate opportunities with some vision, and professional. Remember that they are representing your company's image internationally.

Successful international businesses

I would like to end this section with the most impressive examples of very successful international sales professionals I have encountered so far.

Steve Yeager, president of Medicool Inc., a US manufacturer of various insulin protector cases, is an example of a successful international trader. My company was assisting Medicool and some Arabian companies in becoming business partners. I have not met Steve in person, but through our fax and phone communication we have developed a strong relationship that will last beyond business. This impression is also shared by the Arabian businessmen. Steve has the following magical tools which attract business:

- A welcoming attitude and tone of voice at all times. Keeps his promises and agreements, both written and spoken ones.
- Honesty in informing all parties of the steps and decisions he had taken, even when he did not have to do so.
- Knowledge about the culture of his Arabian clients (even small details).

- In phone communications, his interest goes beyond discussing business only to include other subjects such as geography, traditions, history, and archeological discoveries.
- Asking for, listening, understanding, and appreciating feedback from all parties.

Developing a trusting relationship is very important in international trading because of geographical distances and dealings with unfamiliar environments. Not every international trader will have the chance to visit all of his overseas clients, so utilizing communication lines, fax, and phone to establish trust and draw business is the best, and possibly only, choice.

Two very successful international companies that I believe train their people very well and choose them carefully are Hewlett Packard and 3M. No matter which employee I am dealing with, from the quotation request stage through to the shipping process, all are very helpful, professional and pleasant. The employees themselves are an incentive to seek business with the company they represent. Although I have knowledge about companies who provide a specific product, I prefer to first check with Hewlett Packard and 3M to see if they carry the product, because it is so easy and rewarding to do business with them.

Chapter 7
Meet Your Clients

This section of the book contains interviews with Arabian businessmen sharing their experiences as importers, agents, and distributors for various products from many countries. I consider this part a treasure of information, so read it carefully and with an open mind.

Al-Bader Trading

"American companies should visualize that their expansion into an international market is like extending their arms and that the fingers represent their agents in every country. If the arm does not provide support to the fingers, how would the fingers function well?"

- Medical & Dental Supplies.
- Company Name : Al-Bader Trading Co. W.L.L
- Year Established : 1960's.
- Country : Kuwait
- Interviewee : Mr. Mohammed Ghassan Homsi
- Title: Manager of Medical & Dental Supplies Division.
- Suppliers countries : Germany, America, Italy, Switzerland and France

Which country do you prefer to deal with and why?

Germany. German companies, after dealing with you for a short period, will become more flexible and supportive of your business. In every German company, there is a regional export manager who visits his clients to meet with them and become more understanding of the psychology and the environment of his/her Arabian business partners. One time, a German *company that we had been dealing with for some time changed their export manager. The new export manager altered the way his company was dealing with us and he tried to base it on business is business system. A misunderstanding in our relationship started to grow. The export manager visited us in Kuwait where he saw how companies deal with their clients and with each other and how the human relationship is the base in these dealings. When the export manager went back to Germany, he started dealing with us using the same successful guidelines the previous export manager had followed.*

When companies only deal with their international clients behind a computer screen without studying the geography, culture, and psychology of their business partners, they are destined to have ineffective communication and misunderstandings. A German export *manager that I admire very much shows a great interest in the human side of the people he meets when he is visiting our region. He memorizes names, nationalities, and fields of work for everyone he deals with. When he meets someone for the first time, he will use his previous contact information to show knowledge about a similar client (nationality, field of work, etc.). This creates an instant* connection between the export manager and his new client. In the Arabian world, eighty percent of any business is based on human relations and the rest on the technical side. This export manager was loved and trusted by everyone and his company has greatly profited from his personable approach.

One day I was surprised by the effect of a German export manager action after he finished visiting us and went back to Germany. During his visit, I took him to meet all of our big clients that bought his products. Before leaving, the export manager requested a list of names and addresses for all of the clients we had visited. Two weeks later while I was meeting with one of my clients, he showed me with joy a thank you letter that he had received from the German export manager. This simple letter had such a good effect on this client that he made it a point to buy products from this German company.

Another good point about German companies is their loyalty and deep respect for the contract with their agents. Even when the agent is not doing well, they try to help him in many ways and give him a number of chances to correct the situation. Changing the agent is the last decision they resort to after exhausting all ways and means trying to help him. On the other hand, Swiss and Italian companies don't seem to have the strong loyalty and deep respect for their agents that exists when dealing with German companies.

What I heard about Swiss companies is that they are very helpful and supportive to their clients. Did you experience that?

Yes, you are right. They are very helpful and supportive to their clients and also very generous and welcoming to their visiting guests, but they don't actually respect the exclusive agreement with their agents. This makes the agent feel insecure, untrusting and leads him to not invest a lot in marketing their products compared to the way markets German products.

Did this affect the sales volume of Swiss products in the Kuwaiti market?

For sure; when I import a product from Switzerland and two weeks later I find out that another company has imported the same product then I, the exclusive agent, will be forced to reduce the product price dramatically and fast so I can avoid an unavoidable big loss. The Kuwaiti market is small and can't absorb large quantities, and besides that, what is their definition of exclusivity and where is their understanding of the agency soul?

What do you mean by the "agency soul"?

The agency soul is the basic mutual understanding that in the first year of the agency, the agent will be actually presenting the product to the market and he might not charge his clients so they can be encouraged to exhibit the product on their shelves without any risk. In the second year of the agency, the orders will start coming steadily, and in the third year the agent will start enjoying the profits of his hard work. The manufacturer granting the agency should have an understanding of the great effort involved and of the stages the agent has to go through. Looking for and pressuring the agent to achieve immediate profits in the first year of the agency agreement is not reasonable.

How about doing business with American companies?

You face a lot of complications when doing business with USA companies. They sometimes start their communication by sending a long questionnaire asking for your sales volume in the last four years, your account number, your marketing budget, your 5 year projection of quantities needed, etc. Maybe this system is acceptable and logical in their USA market, but in our market this form of initial communication is not acceptable or usual. We can offer them our company profile that we have prepared; after all, the targeted market is ours and they should start by understanding the way we do business.

The other thing is that USA companies don't offer a good support system for their agents. A simple procedure such as providing samples becomes a complicated issue where it turns into a quotation and a purchase order. Usually, samples all over the world are provided free of charge. When a company is in the first stages of doing business with a prospective agent charges him for the samples, the agent will question if this company will provide any kind of support and encouragement to do business together. I understand that if the company provides all samples free of charge to all requesting companies the operation will be costly, but they should screen these requesting companies and decide the ones worth sending free samples to.

Do you think that to decide if a company is in the ones worth sending free samples to, the manufacturer or supplier can request a reference list?

Yes, they can do that. American companies can also check with the commercial division in the USA embassy in Kuwait for example. They will have access to information about the agencies the Kuwaiti company has. The benefit of this move is not limited to only deciding if the company is worth free samples, but also if the Kuwaiti company has experiences with similar products and if it is a valid option as an agent. The American company could also visit the Kuwaiti company so they could meet face to face and discuss business.

Of all the American companies you have represented, how many have actually visited you?

Almost none of the companies we represent. The only ones visiting frequently have been German companies. Some American companies have established an office or a subsidiary in one of the GCC countries, where this branch is jointly run by Americans and Arabs. The representatives of this branch office will regularly visit their agents and clients in the neighboring GCC countries and the Middle East in general. This branch covers a wide area in which language, culture, and traditions are similar. Also, because this branch employs people who are from this area, it has an edge over other foreign companies in the market. Because this office or subsidiary is located in the area, visits to clients are more frequent and less expensive. In addition, these branch offices are actually huge warehouses for the American companies in which sales, distribution, and delivery is much faster, cheaper, and more efficient. An example of such an American company is 3M with its subsidiary 3M Gulf in United Arab Emirates.

From your experience with American companies, do they respect the set agreements they have with their agents?

Absolutely, you can expect that from them. They are very cautious and take their time in giving a company their agency and that reflects and proves to you their seriousness and respect for the agreement.

Which companies give excellent support to their agents and distributors?

Again, German companies do that very well. Let us say that you have an urgent need for spare parts. German companies will speed the process of delivering the goods to their agent without even waiting for payment to arrive. Besides showing their agent that they trust him, they know that any delay in providing these spare parts will eventually affect the reputation of the product with the end user. They realize that if their agent was not honest and did not pay them back, they can always replace him, but how can they re-institute the trust of the end user in the product after it has been demolished. Customer satisfaction is their first priority and the deciding factor in all situations. This proves that German companies have a clear vision of where the profit is in the long run.

How about American companies when it comes to the issue of providing support to their agents?

You would almost think that they are absolutely unaware of such issues. Even when it comes to urgent requests for spare parts, they always insist on having payment in advance, as if this small amount of money is more important to them than the reputation of their product and the support of their agent. Insisting on payment in advance is one factor which delays the supply of the needed devices or parts. The other factor is the slow response you will face in answering your requests and correspondence, let alone the run-around you may encounter when you must communicate with many departments that sometimes don't know about the subject you are referring to. It seems that American companies have become a collection of specialized departments that have weak and ineffective communication, which frustrates the one who deals with them. I don't understand the wisdom nor see the profit in having a system that will take ten days to respond that the spare parts you have ordered are ready to ship after receiving payment. I am not objecting here to the payment in advance, which is another issue. I am objecting to the time it takes to get an answer for such a simple but crucial order.

What do German companies use that gives them an edge over American companies in providing better and faster support to their agents?

When dealing with German companies, you will notice that they have some form of centralization in the export department. The export department is the only one you need to communicate with; it handles all issues related to its agents without wasting time waiting for other departments to respond. It also seems that German companies give more authority to their employees in making decisions compared to American companies. So, German companies employ enough centralization and authority in their export department, while American companies lack these success keys.

I have heard the same suggestion from many of my Arab clients for the need to have flexibility in payments. Could you expand on this subject? And what do German companies do to ensure that their new client or agent is worth the risk involved in facilitating the payment method?

German companies give their clients the option of payment 120, 90, or 60 days from the date of the invoice. They understand that if a Kuwaiti company is involved in a government tender, it will receive its money 3 months after delivering the goods. Most German companies don't even charge interest on deferred payments, and many of them would facilitate the option of an open account when the value of the goods is less than 5,000DM. This flexibility creates a good atmosphere of loyalty, trust, and cooperation between the company and its agent.

I understand that some agents and companies might abuse the flexibility in payment methods and others might be financially weak and unable to fulfill their obligations and pay their debts, and that's why many companies ask for their money in advance. German companies avoid being in a risky situation by visiting their prospective agents and observing their interactions with other companies and their reputation with the end user. They also observe the staff and the management, which gives them an indication of how well this company will perform as an agent. German companies sign an agency agreement with a company only after studying the company.

Another way German companies can get information about a foreign company is through a German association of German exporters and international traders. The association collects information about foreign companies that trade with or represent German companies. The information will include which German companies the foreign business represents, and if there have been any complaints against it. We purchase gold that is used in dental work from a German company using their currency, the Deutsche Mark. Although sometimes they have faced a loss because of the increase in gold prices in the world, they have never asked us to carry the loss. On the other hand, one time an *American company sent us an invoice for $26 with a note saying that they had made a mistake in the first invoice and we needed to pay the difference, which was $26. Because the amount of the invoice was very small, the employee who* *received it in our department thought that it made more sense to add the $26 to the next order we placed with the American company, especially knowing that the cost of making a money transfer would exceed the amount being transferred. After some time, we received another invoice from the American company for the $26 and $1.07 interest for the delay in not paying it ! The cost of the stamp to send the reminder was more than $1.07.* From my experience, it seems that American companies deal with their clients through a computer, which never makes you feel that you are a valuable customer nor can it establish a human relationship with you.

Companies should know that their agents are not their products' end users, they are their partners. American companies should visualize that their expansion into an international market is like extending their arms and that the fingers represent their agents in every country. If the arm does not provide support to the fingers, how would the fingers function well? Support and good communication between the American manufacturer and their agents is crucial to achieve success.

Some German companies that we represent exhibit an intelligent understanding that the marriage between them and their agents might not be forever. They also understand that the agent can be changed, but when they invest their time and efforts with the current agent they are actually investing in the reputation and marketing of their products. As an example, a German company would sponsor a seminar in the foreign market and the agent would organize the seminar, inviting all of his clients.

What about the quality of US products?

Products that are truly manufactured in the USA still stand for high quality in our market. With certain goods, there is growing concern whether a product that we intend to import from the United States was actually manufactured there or if it was originally imported from the Fareast and re-exported.

One time we imported disposable medical items from an American company under the impression that they were made in the USA. When the shipment arrived, we discovered that what was printed on the cartons was "California, USA", while on the products inside labels the printing read "Made in Pakistan". We had to sell the product on the market at a loss. We are aware that a number of American companies either have or associate with manufacturing facilities in countries where labor costs are low. Still, we notice that the quality is not equal to products made in the USA.

Vision International

"Intensive competition accompanied by the absence of any restrictions on foreign imports is a major feature of the Kuwaiti market. Only goods of high quality and competitive nature will survive"

- Food Products.
- Company Name: Vision International Trading Center
- Year Established: 1991.
- Country: Kuwait
- Interviewee : Mr. Mohammad Al-Hassem
- Title: Manager Managing Director.
- Suppliers countries : USA, Poland, India and Pakistan

Introduce your company to us

Vision International is an import/export and trading firm specializing in importing and marketing selected products from various countries. Our main interest is food products. At the beginning from 1991 until 1993, we were mainly importing and distributing products in Kuwait. In 1993, we started seriously the search to be agents for the products we sell.

What made you decide to acquire agencies?

To guarantee the continuation of the products we sell in Kuwait. By only relying on an import relationship, there is no guarantee that the supplier will always be able to provide us with the products. Having a commitment between our company and the supplier through an agency agreement solves this problem.

What kind of food products did your company introduce to the Kuwaiti market?

We have successfully introduced jams and preserves from Poland, biscuits and cookies from Italy, and tea from India. We also import rice from Pakistan under our own private label, and we are the sole agent for the US based company, Ralston Purina, in the pet food category.

Describe the market you serve?

At this time we serve the Kuwaiti market, which enjoys fairly high purchasing power, thus creating considerable demand for fine quality and durable consumer goods. Actually, Kuwait has one of the highest per-capita levels of imports in the world. Total imports amount to $4,938 million per year.

Intense competition accompanied by the absence of any restrictions on foreign imports is a major feature of the Kuwaiti market. Only goods of high quality and competitive nature will survive. The price/quality relationship of the product is the only decisive factor in its successful marketing in Kuwait. A poor price/quality relationship will cause serious difficulties and eventually a decline in the products share of the market.

How do you locate foreign companies that you want to represent?

We do our search for such companies in Kuwait through references such as the American Export Register that is available from the Kuwaiti chamber of commerce. Another reference source is trade magazines that are available at the Unites States embassy in Kuwait. We also attend a number of trade shows in Germany and business visits to many countries.

Any comments in regard to initial communication with US companies?

Yes. Initial communication coming from USA companies indicates that they base their evaluation on the history and the size of the company seeking the agency. Although the number of years a company has been in the market and its size are important factors in granting agency representation, you should look for a company that will market your product. In our market, it is not always true that a very well known and well established company will be your best choice as an agent. Many of these big or old companies have many agencies that they depend on to survive and dedicate their marketing efforts to. At the same time, these companies also have and continuously acquire new agencies that will not reach beyond their files. So, the size and history of a company does not guarantee the success of the representation. It is actually the opposite. If a company is relatively young and carries few products that might mean that this company will pay more attention and provide greater marketing efforts for the new product.

A US manufacturer gave our company, which is relatively small but aggressive, a line of its products; at the same time it gave another Kuwaiti company, which is big and old, another line of products. Our company's performance surpassed the performance of the big Kuwaiti company and the USA manufacturer offered us an agency for the other line of products. The other Kuwaiti agent already represented a similar product of another brand that he had been selling successfully in the market for a long time, and hence he was not interested in the new brand to the degree that it would compete with the other well established one. His philosophy was that this category of products is doing well and they should direct their marketing efforts toward other categories.

Did your company accept the offer of the USA manufacturer to carry their other line of products?

No, we did not accept their offer. The product appeal with the consumer was affected negatively. We can't present this product as a new one after it has been sitting on supermarket shelves for a long time collecting dust and passing the expiration date. The way you present the product to a new market for the first time is very important in achieving appeal, recognition, and acceptance with the consumers. We had that against us from the beginning, so we turned down the offer.

What is the reason that some Kuwaiti companies wish to represent other brands of similar products they already sell successfully to the market?

In some cases, the success of the Kuwaiti company in selling similar products is thought of as a paved road of experience to sell the new product. In other cases, it is a monopoly. The Kuwaiti company is afraid that if another company wins the agency of the new brand, this new brand might compete against their well-known brand in the market; hence they will be aggressive to win the agency and guarantee that it will not compete with them for the duration of the agency agreement and maybe more.

For example, *I contacted a manufacturer in regard to representing a line of their products that I knew did not exist in our market. The reply came back that this line of products is already represented in Kuwait. Further communication yielded that the manufacturer admits that although his product has an agent in Kuwait, the agent is not marketing or selling it. The manufacturer can't do anything to correct this situation because of the binding agency agreement he had signed with the Kuwaiti company.*

Because of the small size and age of your company, did you face a lot of rejections from foreign companies that you were looking to represent?

Yes, many times. The questionnaire the foreign company requests us to complete asks for bank statements, sales volume, annual number of letters of credit, etc. These kinds of questions are considered a private matter in our market. In addition, are the answers to these questions an indication that the company will perform an excellent job in marketing and selling the products? Not always, and the real example I gave to you is a proof.

From your experience, which companies use a questionnaire as a deciding factor in granting representations?

Mostly USA based companies. Companies from other countries are more flexible, and will usually give you a trial period. Your performance would be the deciding factor for the agency continuation.

What other difficulties do you face with foreign companies?

Two issues come to mind, over-pricing and unreasonable expectations for sales volume. Our market is small, competitive, and experienced with every source of products in the world. Pricing should be decided by studying similar products in the market. You can use your agent as an information source for such data or you can visit the market yourself. The same applies to the expected sales volume. Sometimes the forecasted sales volume is unreasonable for such a small market. I feel that either they are using the wrong sources to obtain market data, or they set unreasonable expectations due to the fact that the GCC countries are wealthy. If the latter is the case, then they should know that wealthy does not mean absence of price shopping. Wealthy means that GCC countries have very educated consumers when it comes to the subject of price/quality relationship because they compare all sorts of products from many different resources around the world.

I hope that the small size of our Kuwaiti market does not weaken the interest of American companies in it. Because of the strong communication network that exists among all Arabian countries, the product that starts in one part will be the launching base for its expansion to the whole region. When I was studying in the United States, I admired very much the way American companies pay equal attention to having their products available in small and large supermarkets. Why not apply the same successful philosophy to international markets? After all, the world is becoming a small place and any expansion into a new market is an expansion to your sales and profits.

Some foreign companies expect their agents to sell big quantities of the products shortly after signing the agency agreement. It seems that these foreign companies missed the point that this is a new market. Did they forget that it took them some time and probably years until their sales in the market reached the current volume? And why don't they expect the same sales development nature with the new market?

Which countries are easier to do business with?

Eastern Europe and the Far East are much easier to do business with. Their slogan is "let's do business" and they are open and very courageous to make the move. With American companies it feels like there is something holding them back. It might be due to the lack of information about our markets and business opportunities.

Could you give me an example of a very successful USA company in the Kuwaiti market? And why is it successful?

There are many. Take, for example, Pepsi. This American company gives great support to their Kuwaiti agent in marketing and advertising. You will notice that many of the small supermarkets that are found all around Kuwait have the Pepsi logo in their signs. As part of their continuous advertisement campaign, Pepsi has authorized their agent to approach every new supermarket and offer to make their sign, with the condition of adding the Pepsi logo to it. The effect of this aggressive and continuous campaign is obvious. The sales of Pepsi Cola surpass any other competitor.

Who should decide the best advertising methods in this market, the foreign company or its agent?

It should be a joint effort. Most Kuwaiti companies don't have the experience or the professional staff to develop creative advertisement campaigns; thus the need for input from the foreign company is important. On the other hand, some advertisement methods and contents might not be suitable for our local market, so the foreign company needs the input of its agent in regard to general guidelines.

Take, for example, advertising for pet food using supermarket displays. Because of cultural reasons, you should not place the pet food display in the front section of the supermarket where it is in the face of the consumer. You can place the display next to the pet food section where it will be more acceptable.

Some advertising methods are not allowed in our market. For example, you can't have in your advertisement a comparison between your product and another product in the market. Also, you can't use sexual innuendo to sell your product.

From you experience, what makes a product attractive to the Kuwaiti consumer? And what makes a product go into high demand?

As I mentioned before, the price/quality relationship is a major factor for the Kuwaiti consumer. Another important factor is the quality of the product packaging. Kuwaiti consumers are very picky and they will judge the product by the way it looks. If the packaging looks cheap or weak, they will not give its contents any chance to prove otherwise.

Kuwaiti consumers are not risk takers when it comes to trying a new brand name. They will be loyal to the product they have used for a long time. You can look at this loyalty in two ways. One is that you have to make your new product very appealing to the consumer by ensuring that the new product has a competitive price, high quality, and good appearance. The other point you should draw from consumers' loyalty is that the minute your product is accepted by the consumers, it will enjoy a long relationship with them.

Word of mouth is another important means of increasing product demand. Our community structure results in a very strong and big communication network. When a product presents itself in a unique way, it will attract the attention of the few that will generate the attention of everyone. Take, for example, the use of supermarket displays to market a product. Some business people believe this idea is not effective for our market because most people avoid these displays for cultural reasons. These business people missed the point that some consumers will try the sample exhibited in the display. These few consumers are actually gateways for your product to the word-of-mouth network.

What weaknesses exist in Kuwaiti companies?

In many companies, you find weak management and lack of customer service. There is almost no attention to the importance of employee training and its effect on company productivity. There is almost no mechanism for customer follow-up or feedback. There is a need to educate sales people in techniques to gain and keep customers.

In Kuwait, for example, notice the difference in management, product display, and customer service between Sultan Center supermarkets, which belong to a private company, and the co-operative supermarkets, which are supervised by a government body. Without any doubt, Sultan Center provides an excellent atmosphere for its shoppers and reflects an intelligent management. In most co-operative supermarkets the only thing that exists are the products themselves, missing any kind of appealing display and customer service. A problem we face as consumer product providers is that 80% of our market exists in co-operative supermarkets.

What other problems do you face as a consumer product agent when dealing with co-operative supermarkets?

Each co-operative supermarket is run by a board of directors elected by the residents of the nearby area. The elected members are also residents of the same area. These members generally don't have any business background, which means that management will most likely be unprofessional and weak. Furthermore, the management receives a set salary that is not related to the sales volume, so there is no incentive to improve sales or service.

To introduce a product to a co-operative supermarket you have to be very patient and persistent. Let's assume that I just became an agent for a consumer item and I need to sell it through a co-operative supermarket. First you have to present the product to the purchasing manager or the purchasing committee who will review it and pass it to the general manager for approval. This step will take around a month. Then the matter will be forwarded to the purchasing department and a date will be set to meet with the agent in 1 to 2 months. A price comparison committee will compare your prices with similar products. Sometimes the new product will be refused because of its price, without giving it the chance to show up on the shelves and test its acceptance with the consumers. If your product is accepted by all of these committees and departments, you can start supplying it to the supermarket.

Foreign companies that carry consumer items and are interested in entering the Kuwaiti market should know the time and effort the agent will need to introduce the product.

Getting your product in the supermarkets is just the beginning. If I want to know if the supermarket needs more quantities of my products, the management will refer me to the worker who organizes my products on the shelves. This worker makes the decision in this matter! If the worker damages some of my products or if the expiration date on my products in the supermarket's warehouse has passed, I will be the one carrying this loss, not the supermarket!

In regard to food products, what are the labeling regulations in your market?

There should be a label on the product that states the production date, the expiration date, and the contents, all written in Arabic. Food items must be tested in government labs to get acceptance for contents and it usually takes around a month to get the results of the test. You must also provide a list of contents to the ministry of commerce for their approval.

Al-Shafei Establishment

"My relationship with my Taiwanese and Italian suppliers from the beginning was more than business. When we visit each other, it is not only heads of business that meet but also our families. Because of that, business was established on strong ties and mutual trust that was built on human interaction. When business starts with such human relationship you will see that trust and loyalty are established faster than waiting for its creation using a business only interaction."

- Medical equipment, physically challenged equipment, hospital furniture, laboratories supplies, educational aid supplies.
- Company Name : Al-Shafei Establishment
- Year Established: 1983
- Country: Saudi Arabia
- Interviewee: Mr. Ahmed Al-Shafei
- Title: Executive Director
- Suppliers' countries: Taiwan, Italy, USA and other countries

Why don't you have any agencies? How do you guarantee a continuous relationship with your suppliers?

I prefer not to have agencies. The two major suppliers I deal with are Taiwanese and Italian companies which don't sell to anyone else other than me in this market.

What kind of agreement do you have with your suppliers?

You can call it a virtual agency or a mutual obligation. I don't buy from anyone else, and they supply only me.

How was that accomplished?

My relationship with my Taiwanese and Italian suppliers from the beginning was more than business. When we visit each other, it is not only heads of business that meet but also our families. Because of that, business was established on strong ties and mutual trust that was built on human interaction. When business starts with such human relationship you will see that trust and loyalty are established faster than waiting for its creation using a business only interaction.

Do you seek the friendship-business relationship with your foreign suppliers?

Yes, as much as I can. Friendship ties ensure that business problems are either nonexistent or solved in a friendly atmosphere. It also adds a sense that you and your supplier are looking after each others' interest. The system I prefer is let's first be friends and then we will do business forever.

You mentioned that you have a friendship-business relationship with your Taiwanese and Italian suppliers. Was the effort to create such a relationship mutual?

Yes, it was. Taiwanese and Italian companies make an effort to get to know their clients beyond only business. *Take, for example, when I visited a Taiwanese company for the first time. Their hospitality was evident throughout my entire visit. They took care of my accommodations, meals, tours, and everything else. Although I had informed them that I was coming to check their market and to take a look at their products, it did not make a difference to them. I still was treated as if I came to actually buy from* them. It is obvious to me that they treat all of their clients, big or small, with the same hospitality and warmth, regardless if this client is only browsing or actually buying. They make you feel as if you are their only client.

You are an Arab and generosity is a distinctive part of your culture. What is the effect of this treatment on you as a businessman?

The generosity and warmth they treat me with is like a debt. This Taiwanese company manufactures wheelchairs. There are many producers of such products in the world and it would take a long time and much effort to compare all of them, but the hospitality of this Taiwanese company made my decision easier. I currently market and sell their products.

Beside the hospitality of this Taiwanese company, what other factors do you like when dealing with them?

They are easy to negotiate with. There is no fixed price concept. They ask for and really listen to my input in regard to market-acceptable pricing and product specifications. They even provide me with the service of actually including with their shipment to me products that I purchased from other Taiwanese companies. They make it easy for me to do business and harder for me to even think of dealing with someone else.

How about your experience with Italian companies?

From my personal experience with a number of Italian companies, I find it easy to do business with them because of the resemblance I noticed between our culture and theirs. The business relationship progresses beyond business because of the warmth both of our cultures have, which leads to a trusting relationship and a flourishing business.

How about your experience with American companies?

I want first to acknowledge that I had fewer experiences with American companies than with others.

One time I paid a visit to a Saudi distributor for an American manufacturer of medical devices. The Saudi distributor is a friend of mine, and I informed him that there was a foreign supplier for a product he distributes who was coming into the market with the same brand he represents at a much lower price. I knew that this friend of mine would appreciate this information and would adjust his price in order to continue to be the supplier of this product. He thought that his price was very competitive especially since he was the distributor for the manufacturer. While I was in his office, he called the American manufacturer's representative and asked him to explain how there could be another supplier with a better price. The American representative very arrogantly replied that the new supplier was selling from an old stock and that it was a temporary situation. I responded that it was not temporary and that the new foreign supplier was not selling an old stock. I knew what I was talking about, but the American representative showed that he was not even interested in listening to his own clients. Of course, they were forced after some time to reduce their prices in order to compete with the new market reality.

I would like to describe a different experience with *one of the well known Japanese companies, National. I met one of their sales managers in an exhibit that was held in Jeddah, Saudi Arabia. I made a comment that one of their medical products that was exhibited was not up to their reputation or to the competition in our market. The product under discussion was a light used by physicians to check the mouth area. I invited the Japanese sales manager to visit my showroom and check a competitive product that was manufactured in Taiwan. I was shocked and impressed one day when the Japanese sales manager and six of his associates visited me. They were very interested in what I had to say, taking notes and pictures of the competitive*

Taiwanese product. Their local Saudi distributor was accompanying them in their visit. They knew that the information I could provide them was valuable and could not be obtained from their local agent because he was a wholesaler, while my company was in direct sales to the end users. They asked me for suggested improvements to the light and of the right pricing for the market. What a difference between National's sales manager's reaction and the American manufacturer's representative.

How about the quality of American products?

The quality of American products, in the eyes of importers and consumers, is in doubt. From experience, we know that many American products are manufactured outside the United States. In this case, as an importer I prefer to buy directly from the manufacturing source; this will save me money and save my reputation in the market by presenting products that without a doubt are made in the country I am claiming to my customers. Personally, to avoid being in this situation, I always request a sample from the American company so I can be sure that I will be buying a truly American-made product.

On the other hand, European, Italian, and Japanese products still hold a place of quality as fine products with lower prices than the American ones. I have also noticed that Taiwanese quality has improved in competition with Japanese-made products.

What is your advice for a foreign company searching for a Saudi representative?

My personal opinion is that the foreign company should not go after big names in our market because it is not an indication that their selection is the most effective one. In this case, the foreign company's product will not be the agent's main interest. They should go after smaller companies that will depend greatly on the success of the new product in the market. Go after the smaller, more eager companies for business. Do not make your existence in the new market confined to a piece of paper (the distribution agreement) in your new Saudi representative's files. As a foreign company, when you receive the profile of a company looking to represent your products, check to see how many other products they represent. This will tell you if they will be able to give your products enough attention.

Another reason for not only considering old big companies to represent you is that usually the heads of management in these companies are not active in developing the skills of their marketing and sales people. Most of them are still doing business using old and ineffective systems that lack progress and improvement.

The foreign company should also be aware that they are entering a new market and placing unreasonable conditions or expectations will be a hindrance to success. One time a foreign manufacturer expressed that they would grant me their business on the condition that my yearly purchases from them should not be less than 2 million Saudi Riyals. Their condition was unreasonable and uneducated especially knowing that their products had not yet been introduced to our local market. It goes without saying, communication stopped and cooperation was killed before it even started. By the way, this was a Canadian company.

There is another point the foreign company should be aware of, although it might be difficult to detect. They should be sure that their agency is granted to a Saudi company that is truly run by a Saudi citizen. Although by law a Saudi company should be truly run by its Saudi owner, in many cases this might not be true.

You will find that some companies are actually run by a foreigner. The point here is that you will be granting your agency and business to a person who might one day be unable to conduct business in Saudi Arabia. Another point is that when you are dealing with a truly Saudi-run business, you are at least sure that the owner feels more responsible to conduct his business in a legal way because he is working in the environment he will always reside in.

It is also very important and beneficial that you visit the market and meet with your prospective clients. In this way you can establish a better relationship with your clients, understand the market, and be able to make educated and more accurate decisions and choices.

What are the qualities a visiting international representative should have in order to succeed in his mission in your market?

He should be humble and sensitive to the culture he is visiting. Even if you as an international representative were from the number one country in the world or the number one company in the world, your mission is to make deals and understand the target market, not to treat others as if you are somehow superior. You also have to be a good listener and a flexible negotiator.

Describe your market and what is needed to succeed in it as an agent for a foreign company?

Our market is an open market with intense competition. Price plays an important role in the success of a product. As an agent, you definitely need the backup of the foreign business you represent.

Take, for example, a Canadian medical device that was expensive in comparison with other similar products in the market. The price in this case was not a deterrent because the manufacturer backed up the product with a guarantee that if the device malfunctioned the consumer could return the unit to the Saudi distributor, pay a small fee and receive a new unit. With this kind of warranty for the product, consumers overlooked its high price. After some time though, the manufacturer no longer honored the warranty and the reputation of the product went down and so did sales. It seems that the high volume sales blinded the Canadian company, who underestimated the importance of consistency and the role of a good backup plan in continuing to seize the market.

The purchasing power that exists in Saudi Arabia is big. Consumption of consumer products is high. Our market also has a unique characteristic related to the pilgrimage to Mecca, where 2 million consumers from all over the world are temporarily added to the population. In a period of two months every year sales of goods, especially consumer goods, sharply increases. In my business field, for example, stethoscopes, blood pressure measuring devices and diabetic equipment goes into high demand during the pilgrimage season. Because our market is an open market, pilgrims benefit from the wide variety and selections of goods. Sales of toys, gift items, umbrellas, clothing, and food also increase sharply during these two months.

Take the following success story. It is a fact that our market lacks in good customer service, a follow up plan and marketing skills. *A Saudi car dealer who sells Toyota, a Japanese car, has recently taken over the management in his father's company. Sales of his cars increased dramatically, reaching 700 cars a month. The changes this manager put in place were bringing new sales and marketing staff that was professionally trained in the newly opened training center. He also introduced a new concept to the market, facilitating buying a car without a down payment. The most noticeable change in the eyes of the customers was the professional and courteous treatment they received from this dealership. Word of mouth took care of spreading the news.*

Some foreign businessmen complain that some Arabian businessmen are hard to read when it comes to measuring the degree of their interest in the subject under discussion. What's your opinion?

In some cases, this statement is true. To overcome this situation, the foreign businessman should stress the fact that any feedback or suggestions in regard to all aspects of the subject under discussion be it the pricing, specifications, or conditions set forth, are all welcomed and negotiable. If the foreign businessman exhibits inflexibility and uneasiness in negotiating, he is actually shutting the door to a two-way communication.

Do not pressure your prospective Arabian business partner into giving you an instant decision. Be aware that Arabs are cautious at the beginning, but once trust is established, mutual business will be conducted in a friendly, warm, and honest atmosphere.

Most businesses in our market are owned and run by families and a decision cannot be made until other family members are consulted. Sometimes the consultation is crucial to the decision and sometimes it is a sign of respect to other family members. Business, although important, doesn't run the way its members interact; traditions and the human side controls part of the business structure.

Should the majority of Arabian companies which can be described as a family business keep this form, or should they change it to expand their base by having shareholders and an elected board of directors?

My personal opinion is that we should keep the family business form because of many reasons related to our social structure. First, as you know, we are a family oriented society that strongly encourages the unity of the family structure, both the immediate and the extended. I consider this a very positive and good characteristic of our society that we should preserve and encourage, because of the many benefits it delivers to the nation and the individual. Our traditions and religion always encourage and emphasize the importance of this social behavior.

Abana Enterprises

"To understand anyone's culture and environment you have to actually not only live in the geographical location but also mix with the people and interact with them on a daily basis. You will not get a grasp on understanding a country and its people by staying in the Sheraton or the Hilton for few days."

- Bank Automation Systems, Security Systems and other various projects.
- Company Name: Abana Enterprises
- Year Established: 1970
- Country: Saudi Arabia
- Interviewee: Mr. Abdulrahman Al-Jebreen
- Title: Executive Director
- Suppliers' countries: USA, Germany, France, Japan, Italy.

Introduce your company to us

In 1970 I started importing cars, sleeping bags and water coolers from the United States to the Saudi market. I chose American made products because I had been a student in the United States studying business administration. In 1978, Abana was completely involved in agriculture, an old interest of mine. I had a degree from the agriculture college in Saudi Arabia. My business field corresponded with the strong interest and support the Saudi government put forward in agriculture at that time.

Abana became the first agriculture consulting office in Saudi Arabia. We also had established a number of greenhouses.

In 1984, we realized the growing problem of water shortages and also started to shift our interest into another avenue, telecommunications. In 1986, we established a branch specializing in bank automation and equipment.

From your extensive experience what are the weaknesses that exist in Saudi companies?

There is a concentration of interest on top management and less interest is placed on the support to management positions, such as marketing and sales. We perform very few market studies, and even when they exist, the results of these studies are rarely implemented.

There are companies that specialize in conducting market research and feasibility studies, but the problem with using their services is the fear that some of these consulting companies might steal your project and invest in it. As you know, a person can be involved in different types of businesses at the same time.

A consulting firm that has other investments and businesses in the market is actually exhibiting a conflict of interest; we still need some kind of regulation or organization for business in such situations.

Because of the intense competition and recent changes in the Saudi market do you think that market research and feasibility studies will become a necessary tool for every business?

Yes. Currently, more educated businessmen are aware of the increasing importance of such tools to their businesses; some of them are trying to establish in-house market research and studies departments. Depending on consulting firms to perform a market research or a feasibility study, besides its being a risk in some cases, actually sometimes will cost more than testing the idea on a small scale.

What are the difficulties that face Saudi companies?

Companies that deal directly with small distributors and consumers face the problem of collecting their money. In other countries there are collection agencies that will do this job. In our market, small and medium sized companies perform this time, money, and effort consuming task themselves.

Another difficulty Saudi companies' face is the complications they go through to obtain professional and qualified management, sales, marketing, or accounting foreign employees. It is a very consuming and complicated issue. The company will be running around in bureaucracy circles to obtain the visas. When a foreign employee starts working in the Saudi company it is very difficult to fire him, even if it is proved that he is not qualified enough to do the job.

The company has already spent money and great efforts to bring this employee to its work force, which will be a discouragement to get rid of him and find a replacement. Even if the Saudi company found a qualified foreign worker residing in Saudi Arabia, the process of changing his visa papers and status is complicated and time consuming.

Why do companies search for non-Saudi employees to fill the marketing and sales divisions?

The problem lies in the psychology of some Saudis who hold a degree in marketing and sales. There is a tendency to directly seek management positions without trying to first get the experience needed by working in lower level jobs like front sales. Some who have an established family business find it inappropriate and useless to start from the bottom, while they can directly hold a higher position in the company.

Of course, this way of thinking is slowly changing as the society's view of front line jobs is changing. That's why there is a current need to fill these positions with foreign workers.

The old generation of companies came to existence with a very rapid and huge wealth because of the early economic boom in the GCC countries and especially Saudi Arabia. Some business people think that these companies are not up to the job in the new market reality, and that companies should change form from their family owned businesses to a more extended base?

First, I would like to disagree with the way some people view the older generation of businessmen. It is true that part of the old generation of businessmen did not have any experience in business but were lucky in benefiting from the early economic boom in the Saudi market. You will see that some of these businessmen don't have an educated way of managing their businesses and most of the time decisions are made on an emotional basis.

On the other hand, a large percentage of the old generation of businessmen has extensive experience that existed prior to the economic boom. These businessmen have my utmost respect and admiration. They were able to survive and function well when the market was tough in the old days. They have valuable experience and knowledge in business, and their current success did not come from emptiness.

I am 100% against the continuation of the old business structure being confined to a family. The new market reality calls for group work, not individuality. Business should not be based only on emotions. It is becoming a necessity for business continuation and survival in our market to extend beyond confinement to a family. A new business structure is now a necessity, not a choice.

Some foreign businessmen complain that some Arabian businessmen show a lot of interest in doing business during the initial stages but the interest does not materialize into an actual cooperation. Is that true? And if so, how to handle it?

Yes, it is true. Some Arabian businessmen get excited about a product or a business idea. Their initial interest is genuine and sincere although it might not materialize. Take me, for example; I might attend an exhibit and see a product that I believe will be suitable for my market, but when I go back to my company and sit down with my associates and financial manager, I discover that we can't carry this product for one reason or another. In some cases, I might be initially unaware of certain restrictions and regulations that surround this business project or product; it might take my company up to 3 months to research the feasibility of such a venture.

Emotion plays a role in our business decisions, although we know that emotion might yield inaccurate business decisions. Personally, I respond within a week about the decision we made or the current status of our interest, and I believe that is an obligation we must fulfill toward the foreign company.

If you are a representative of a foreign company either in a trade show or visiting a foreign market to locate a business partner or an agent or a distributor, your time and the cost associated with your efforts are, of course, very valuable to you. To avoid feeling frustrated and to weed out the not-so-serious businessmen you will meet with, I suggest that your company should have a procedure that in order to hold discussions with other companies about the same product, the client you are meeting with should put forward a non-refundable deposit. In this way your time is not wasted and seriously interested companies are recognized.

I heard many complaints about dealing with USA companies and the many complications that exist. Is that true in your own experience?

No, in my own experience, it is the opposite. The best companies I ever dealt with are American companies. Over the last 20 years, I had only two bad experiences with American companies. I know that some Arabian companies are sensitive toward certain requests initiated by American companies, like asking for a financial statement. I think that this request is normal and should not be construed as an inquiry for private information. These kinds of requests made by American companies are not geared only toward Arabian companies but also toward other American companies.

You might notice that German or Italian companies don't place such inquiries, but every company has its own procedures in doing business.

I remember one time in 1982 I was experiencing financial difficulties. An American company I was communicating with at that time asked for a financial statement. I did not hide the truth about my difficult financial situation, and to my surprise the American company did not back down and we worked things out.

In my experience, American companies will not only evaluate you based on your financial statement. They appreciate honesty and truthfulness.

From your extensive dealings with American companies, could you give some suggestions on how to better the partnership?

Company polices should be more flexible and accommodating to the specific market they are dealing with. There are obvious differences between the Arabian market and the American market and between the Arabian market and the European market. Company polices should take these differences into consideration.

There is a shortage of support given by some American companies to their Arab agents. I know that this shortage is not intentional, but I think American companies use the same support measurements for different markets and that is not appropriate.

I would like to also to stress the need for more patience from American companies for their Arabian partners before and after they sign the contract. You can't expect your Saudi partner to operate in the same matter as an American business. Take, for example, the slow communication speed; try not to be annoyed by it or translate it as a sign of negligence.

We are different in culture, laws, regulations, and environment. In the United States, if a company needs an operations manager they can advertise for their need, while in Saudi Arabia it is a more complicated and time-consuming issue. In the United States, bills are paid through the mail, while in the Arabian world almost everything has to be hand delivered.

Also medium and small size companies in the Arabian market do not get support from local banks, while in the United States they have a lot of bank support. All of these differences should be put in perspective. The Saudi businessman in my opinion is very serious, hard working, and dedicated but do not place expectations on him that do not correspond with his work environment.

To understand anyone's culture and environment you have to actually not only live in the geographical location, but also mix with the people and interact with them on a daily basis. You will not get a grasp on understanding a country and its people by staying in the Sheraton or the Hilton for few days. What I always suggest to my American business partners is to place one of their employees in my company so he could be their eyes, ears, and window to understanding the current market situation and what their Arabian agent is performing and going through.

Chapter 8

Windows to Understanding the People & Their Culture

This section contains translated Arabian proverbs, which are windows to knowing and understanding the Arabs and their culture. An explanation is added whenever further clarification is needed. I personally enjoy knowing the proverbs of any culture because they give me insights as to what shapes its people. Proverbs also contain the experiences and wisdom of many generations. I am sure that you will find some of these proverbs match proverbs from your culture. After all, we are all humans and have similar experiences.

➢ **For an eye a thousand eyes are honored.**

The eye here refers to people. Because of one person who is very loved, respected and appreciated, for his sake a thousand people will be honored. Honored here also means helped. In short, a person will help another person whom he does not directly know because both of them know a third person at the same time. This is a form of communication which is used to speed and facilitate solving problems and getting help

➢ **The one, who offers to give help as a choice, will not give help.**

The meaning is, if someone offers to help someone else by presenting help as a choice, not a must, then this person did not actually offer to help. Asking for help in sensitive issues is usually difficult to do and connected with ones dignity. So when a person offers to help, he/she should be persistent and insist that the person needing the help accepts it. This way the person needing the help is sure that the giver wants to help. This proverb is used to stress the importance of protecting the dignity of the person needing help and to ensure sensitivity in handling the situation.

> **Nothing scratches your back like your nail.**

It means no one is better in fulfilling your needs than yourself.

> **The best talk is short and to the point.**

> **What you do will be done to you.**

> **Let the baker bake your bread even if he eats half of it.**

In short, it is better to assign the work to one who is specialized in it.

> **Me and my brother against our cousin and me and my cousin against the stranger**

This proverb stresses the importance of family ties and family hierarchy.

> **Debt is a worry at night and a humiliation during the day.**

> **To praise one's self is odiousness.**

> **The one with patience is the one that will reach.**

> **The one who lives by artifice will die poor.**

➢ **A promise is an obligation.**

➢ **What's in the heart will be uncovered by the tongue.**

➢ **Be afraid of he who is not afraid of god.**

➢ **The one who does not lose does not gain.**

➢ **The one who does not measure before he dives will not benefit from measuring after diving.**

➢ **Judge a person by his ethics, not by what he wears.**

➢ **If a material object had lasted for someone else, it would not have reached you.**

Don't feel superior to others because of your possessions or position. Neither will last forever. Remember that the person who used to own them before they got to you, could not own them forever.

➢ **Who walks a span toward you, walk a cubit toward him.**

The one who seeks your friendship and treats you well, in return you should treat him even better.

➢ **Humiliate your money not yourself.**

You should spend your money to protect your dignity and honor; don't humiliate yourself for the sake of money.

➢ **The days are longer than its residents.**

It means that days are longer than anyone's life. This proverb is advice to divide one's work into healthy portions so as not to exhaust oneself.

➢ **The one who slanders others in front of you will slander you in front of others.**

Appendixes

Appendix A

International Trade Magazines

Trade & Culture
Published quarterly by Trade & Culture, Inc.
7127 Harford Road
Baltimore, MD 21234-7741
Telephone: (800) 544-5684
Fax: (410) 444-7837

World Trade
Published monthly by Freedom Magazines, Inc.
500 Newport Center Drive, 4th Floor
Newport Beach, CA 92660
Telephone: (714) 640-7070
Fax: (714) 640-7770

Export Today
Published nine times a year by Trade Communications, Inc.
733 15th Street, NW, Suite 1100
Washington, DC 20005
Telephone: (800) 824-9785
Fax : (202) 783-5966

Foreign Trade
Published ten times a year by FT, Inc.
6849 Old Dominion Drive, Suite 200
McLean, VA 22101
Telephone: (703) 448-1338

Traveler, The Business & Travel Magazine for International Traders.
Published monthly by The Asian Sources Media Group
For subscriptions contact :
Wordright Enterprises Inc.,
P.O.Box 3062
Evanston, IL 60204-3062
Telephone: (708) 475-1900
Fax: (708) 475-2794

International Business
Published monthly by American International
Publishing
500 Mamaroneck Avenue
Suite 314
Harrison, NY 10528-9932
Telephone : (800) 274-8187

The Exporter
Published by Trade Data Reports, Inc.
34 West 37th Street
New York, NY 10018
Telephone: (212) 563-2772
Fax: (212) 563-2798

Appendix B

Arabian Newspapers

Arab Times (English)
P.O.Box 2270, Safat 13023, Kuwait

Kuwait Times (English)
P.O.Box 1301, Safat 13014, Kuwait

Gulf Daily News
P.O.Box 5300, Manama, Bahrain

Khaleej Times (English)
P.O.Box 26707, Adliya, Bahrain

Jordan Times
P.O.Box 6710, Amman, Jordan

Times Of Oman
P.O.Box 3770, Ruwi, Oman

Khaleej Times (English)
P.O.Box 6305, Ruwi, Oman

Gulf Times
 P.O.Box 2888, Doha, Qatar

Khaleej Times (English)
P.O.Box 3082, Abu Dhabi, United Arab Emirates

Riyadh Daily (English)
P.O.Box 2943, Riyadh 11476, Saudi Arabia

Al Riyadh
P.O.Box 2943, Riyadh 11476, Saudi Arabia

Appendix C

Arabian Exhibits & Trade Shows Organizers

Riyadh Exhibitions Company
P.O.Box 56010, Riyadh 11554, Saudi Arabia
Tel : (9661) 454-4228
Fax : (9661) 454-4846

Dhahran International Exhibitions
P.O.Box 7519, Dammam 31472, Saudi Arabia
Tel : (9663) 857-9111
Fax : (9663) 857-2285

Al Harithy Company For Exhibitions
P.O.Box 40740, Jeddah 21511, Saudi Arabia
Tel : (9662) 654-6384
Fax : (9662) 654-6853

Kuwait International Fairs Company
P.O.Box 656, Safat 13007, Kuwait
Tel : (965) 245-86501
Fax : (965) 539-3872

Trade Center Management Company
P.O.Box 9292, Dubai, United Arab Emirates
Tel : (9714) 373-300
Fax : (9714) 373-493

Oman International Trade & Exhibitions
P.O.Box 1475, Ruwi 112, Oman
Tel : (968) 564-303
Fax : (968) 565-165

Appendix D

Arabian Banks in the USA

Arab American Bank
40 East 52nd Street, New York, New York 10022
Tel: (212) 644-2000
Fax: (212) 755-6944

Riyadh Bank, Houston Agency
700 Louisiana, Suite 4770, Houston, Texas 77002
Tel: (713) 224-8071
Fax: (713) 224-8072
Head Office: Saudi Arabia

Arab Bank PLC
520 Madison Avenue, New York, NY 10022
Tel: (212) 715-9700
Fax: (212) 223-3175
Head Office: Jordan

Abu Dhabi International Bank Inc
1776 G Street, NW, Suite 850, Washington DC 2006
Tel: (202) 842-7900
Fax: (202) 842-7955
Head Office: United Arab Emirates

Arab Banking Corporation

600 Travis Street, Suite 1900, Houston, TX 77002
Tel: (713) 227-8444
Fax: (713) 227-6507
Head Office: Bahrain

Commercial Bank of Kuwait

19th floor, 350 Park Avenue, New York, NY 10022
Tel: (212) 207-242
Fax: (212) 935-6463
Head Office: Kuwait

Doha Bank Limited

127 John Street, New York, NY 10038
Tel: (212) 509-4030
Fax: (212) 509-6433
Head Office: Qatar

Gulf International Bank BSC

380 Madison Avenue, New York, NY 10017
Tel: (212) 922-2300
Fax: (212) 922-2309
Head Office: Bahrain

National Bank Of Kuwait SAK

299 Park Avenue, 20th Floor, New York, NY 10171
Tel: (212) 303-9800
Fax: (212) 319-8269
Head Office: Kuwait

Saudi International Bank

520 Madison Avenue, New York, NY 10022
Tel: (212) 355-6530
Fax: (212) 702-1045
Head Office: Saudi Arabia

United Bank of Kuwait PLC

Tower 56, 126 East Street, New York, NY 10022
Tel: (212) 832-6700
Fax: (212) 319-4762
Head Office: Kuwait

Appendix E

Desk Officers At The Office of the Near East (International Trade Administration)

Tel: (202) 482-1860
Fax: (202) 482-0878
Flash Facts: (202) 482-1064
http://www.buyusa.gov

Every country in the world is assigned a country desk officer. These desk officers, in Commerce's International Economic Policy (IEP) area, look at the needs of an individual U.S. firm wishing to sell in a particular country, taking into account that country's overall economy, trade policies, political situation, and other relevant factors. Each desk officer collects up-to-date information on the country's trade regulations, tariffs and value-added taxes, business practices, economic and political developments, trade data and trends, market size and growth, and so on. Desk officers also participate in preparing Commerce's country-specific market research reports.

Appendix F

How to Access the National Trade Data Bank

http://www.stat-usa.gov

To subscribe contact:
STAT-USA, Economics & Statistics Administration
US Department Of Commerce
HCHB 4885, Washington, DC 20230
Tel: (202) 482-1986, Fax: (202) 482-2164
E-mail: statmail@esa.doc.gov

Via ordering the CD-ROM version:
STAT-USA's Help Line at (202) 482-1986

Via Federal Depository Libraries: (Free)
You can obtain a list of Federal Depository Libraries in your area by calling the Trade Information Center Fax System at 800-872-8723.

Appendix G

Arab Embassies in the USA

Embassy Of Algeria
2118 Kalorama Road, NW
Washington, DC 20008
Tel : (202) 265-2800

Embassy Of Bahrain
3502 International Drive, NW
Washington, DC 20008
Tel : (202) 342-0741

Embassy Of Egypt
2310 Decatur Pl., NW
Washington, DC 20008
Tel : (202) 232-5400

Embassy Of Jordan
3504 International Drive, NW
Washington, DC 20008
Tel : (202) 966-2664

Embassy Of Kuwait
2940 Tilden Street, NW
Washington, DC 20008
Tel : (202) 966-1897

Embassy Of Lebanon
2560 28th Street, NW
Washington, DC 20008
Tel : (202) 939-6300

Embassy Of Morocco
1601 21st Street, NW
Washington, DC 20008
Tel : (202) 462-7979

Embassy Of Oman
2342 Massachusetts Avenue, NW
Washington, DC 20008
Tel : (202) 387-1980

Embassy Of Qatar
600 New Hampshire Avenue, NW
 Suite 1180
Washington, DC 20037
Tel : (202) 338-0111

The Royal Embassy Of Saudi Arabia
601 New Hamphshire Avenue, NW
Washington, DC 20037
Tel : (202) 342-3800

Embassy Of Sudan
2210 Massachussets Avenue, NW
Washington, DC 20008
Tel : (202) 338-8565

Embassy Of The Syrian Arab Republic

2215 Wyoming Avenue, NW
Washington, DC 20008
Tel : (202) 232-6313

Embassy Of Tunisia
1515 Massachusetts Avenue, NW
Washington, DC 20005
Tel : (202) 862-1850

Embassy Of The United Arab Emirates
600 New Hampshire Avenue, NW
 Suite 74
Washington, DC 20037
Tel : (202) 338-6500

Embassy Of The Republic Of Yemen
2600 Virginia Avenue, NW
 Suite 705
Washington, DC 20037
Tel : (202) 965-4760

Appendix H

Publishers of Business Directories

Kompass Media Sales
2000 Clearwater Drive.
Oak Brook, IL 60521, USA
Telephone : (708) 574-7081
Fax : (708) 574-7080

The Journal Of Commerce
445 Marshall Street.
Phillipsburg, NJ 08865-9984, USA
Telephone : (800) 222-0356
Fax : (908) 454-6507

American Business Information Inc.
5711 South 86th Circle
 P.O.Box 27347
Omaha, NE, USA
Telephone : (402) 593-4565
Fax : (402) 331-6681

Digital Directory Assistance Inc
6931 Arlington Road, Suite 405
Bethesda, MD 20814, USA
Telephone : (800) 284-8353

Appendix I

US International Trade Associations

Monterey Bay International Trade
 Association
725 Front Street, Suite 104
Santa Cruz, CA 95061-0523
Telephone : (408) 469-0148
Fax : (408) 469-0917

Export Managers Association Of California
110 E. Ninth Street, Ste. A-669
Los Angeles, CA 90079
Telephone : (213) 892-1388

American Association Of Exporters And
 Importers
11 W. 42nd Street
New York, NY 10036
Telephone : (212) 944-2230

American Society Of International
 Executives
18 Sentry Parkway, Suite One
Blue Bell, PA 19422
Telephone : (215) 540-2295

Committee For Small Business Exports
 P.O.Box 6
Aspen, CO 81612
Telephone : (303) 925-7567

Federation Of International Trade
Associations
1851 Alexander Bell Drive
Reston, VA 22091
Telephone : (703) 391-6106

International Trade Council
1900 Mt. Vernon Avenue
 P.O.Box 2478
Alexandria, VA 22301-0478
Telephone : (703) 548-1234

International Traders Association
6100 Variel Avenue
Woodland Hills, CA 91367
Telephone : (818) 884-4400

National Association Of Export Companies
 P.O.Box 1330
Murray Hill Station
New York, NY 10156
Telephone : (212) 725-3311
Fax : (212) 725-3312

National Federation Of Export Associations
4865 Cordell Avenue
Bethesda, MD 20814
Telephone : (301) 907-8647

The International Trade Facilitation Council
350 Broadway, Suite 205
New York, NY 10013
Telephone : (212) 925-1400

Overseas Sales And Marketing AssociationsOf America
 P.O.Box 37
Lake Bluff, IL 60044
Telephone : (718) 234-1760

World Trade Centers Association
One World Trade Center, Suite 7701
New York, NY 10048
Telephone : (212) 313-4600

Council For Export Trading Companies
1200 19th Street, N.W., Suite 605
Washington, DC 20036
Telephone : (202) 861-4705

Appendix J

US Embassies in the Arab Countries

Algeria,
 U.S. Embassy
 4 Chemin Cheikh Bachir
 Brahimi (Algiers)
 B.O. Box 549
 16000 Alger
 Telephone : 213-2-601-425
 Fax : 213-2-601-863

Bahrain
 U.S. Embassy
 Bldg. 979, Rd. 3119
 P.O.Box 26431
 Manama, Bahrain
 Telephone : 973-273-300
 Fax : 973-272-594

Jordan
 U.S. Embassy
 P.O.Box 354
 Amman, Jordan
 Telephone : 962-6-644-371
 Fax : 962-6-659-667

Kuwait
 U.S. Embassy
 P.O.Box 77
 Safat 13001, Kuwait
 Telephone : 965-242-4151
 Fax : 965-244-2855

Morocco
 U.S. Embassy
 2 Ave de Marrakech
 P.O.Box 120
 Rabat, Morocco
 Telephone : 212-7-622-65

Oman
 U.S. Embassy
 P.O.Box 50202
 Madinat Qaboos
 Muscat, Oman
 Telephone : 968-698-989
 Fax : 968-699-778

Qatar
 U.S. Embassy
 P.O.Box 2399
 Doha, Qatar
 Telephone : 974-864-701

Saudi Arabia
 U.S. Embassy
 Collector Rd.
 Riyadh Diplomatic Quarter
 P.O.Box 94309
 Riyadh 11693, Saudi Arabia
 Telephone : 966-1-488-3800

Syria
 U.S. Embassy
 Abu Rumaneh
 Al Mansur Strret, No.2
 P.O.Box 29
 Damascus, Syria
 Telephone : 963-11-332-315
 Fax : 963-11-718-687

United Arab Emirates
 U.S. Embassy
 P.O.Box 4009
 Abu Dhabi, UAE
 Telephone : 971-2-345-545
 Fax : 971-2-331-374
Yemen
 U.S. Embassy
 P.O.Box 1088
 San'a, Yemen
 Telephone : 967-2-238-842
 Fax : 967-2-251-563

Egypt
 U.S. Embassy
 5 Sharia Latin America
 Cairo, Egypt
 Telephone : 202-355-8368

Sudan
 U.S. Embassy
 Ali Abdul Latif Street
 P.O.Box 699
 Khartoum, Sudan

Appendix K

Arab Chambers of Commerce in Arab Countries

Algeria Chamber of Commerce
Chambre de Commerce et d'Industrie d'Algiers
11 Chemin Doudou Mokhlar Ben Aknoun
Algiers, Algeria
Tel: (213) 792323
Tx : (0408) 53344 DZ

Bahrain Chamber of Commerce & Industry
P.O. Box 248
King Faisal Highway
Manama, Bahrain
Tel: (973) 233913
Fax: (973) 241294
Tx : (0490) 8691 GHURFA BN

Djibouti
Chambre Internationale de Commerce et d'Industrie
de Djibouti
B.P. 84,
Djibouti, Djibouti
Tel: (253) 351070
Tx : (0979) 5957 DJ

Egypt Chambers of Commerce
Federation of Egyptian Chambers of Commerce
Cairo, Egypt
Tel: (020) 2-3551164/3542943
Tx : (091) 92645 FEDCOC UN

Cairo Chamber of Commerce
4 Midan El- Falaki St.
Cairo, Egypt
Tel: (020) 2-3542943
Tx : (091) 92453 UN

Egyptian Chamber of Commerce of Alexandria
31 Ghorfa Togaria St.
Alexandria, Egypt
Tel: (020) 3-809339/808993/807355

Iraq Chambers of Commerce

Federation of Iraqi Chambers of Commerce
P.O. Box 11348
Mustansir St.,
Baghdad, Iraq
Tel: (964) 1-8888850
Tx : (0491) 212821
Cable: PUBTLS IK

Baghdad Chamber of Commerce
P.O. Box 11348,
Mustansir St.,
Baghdad, Iraq
Tel: (964) 1-8876211

Tx : (0401) 212821 IK

Basrah Chamber of Commerce Aziziyah
Basrah, Iraq
Tel: (964) 40-211343

Mosul Chamber of Commerce
P.O. Box 35
Khalid Ibn Al-Waleed
Mosul, Iraq
Tel: (964) 60-3542/72841/72745

Jordan Chambers of Commerce

Federation of Jordanian Chambers of Commerce
Mr. Amin Husseini, Secretary General
P.O. Box 7029
Amman 11118 Jordan
Tel: (0962) 6-665492 -674495
Fax: (0962) 6-685997
Tlx: (0493) 24103 FJCC JO
Cable: CHAMBERS

Amman Chamber of Commerce
Chairman: Mr. Haider Murad
Director General: Mr. Mohamed Ammar
P.O. Box 287

Amman, Jordan
Tel: (962-6) 666151/4
Fax: (962-6) 666155
Tlx: (493) 21543 CHAM JO

Amman Chamber of Industry
P.O. Box 1800
Amman, Jordan
Tel: (0962) 6-644569
Tx : (0493) 22079
Cable: INDOSJ JO

Kuwait Chamber of Commerce & Industry
Chamber's Building , Ali Salem St.,
P.O. Box 775,
Safat, Kuwait 13008
Tel: (965) 2433864
Fax: (965) 2404110
Tx : (0496) 22198
Cable: GURFTIGARA KT

Lebanon Chambers of Commerce

General Union of Arab Chambers of Commerce,
Industry & Agriculture
P.O. Box 2837-11
Beirut, Lebanon
Tel: (961) 1-814269

Chamber of Commerce & Industry
Mr. Walid Naja, Director General
Justinian Street
P.O. Box 11-1801
Sanayeh 2100,
Beirut, Lebanon
Tel: (961) 1-353390/91/92/93

Fax: (961) 1-602374
Tlx: (0494)22269 CHACIA, (0494)42241 INCO

Libya Chambers of Commerce

Federation of Chambers of Commerce, Industry &
Agriculture
P.O. Box 2321
Tripoli, Libya
Tel: (218) 21-33755
Tx : (0901) 20461 ALGURFALY

Tripoli Chamber of Commerce & Industry &
Agriculture
P.O. Box 2321, 3rd Floor, Dirany Bldg, Boulevard
St,
Tripoli, Libya
Tel: (218) 21-33755
Tx : (0901) 20181

Benghazi Chamber of Commerce, Trade, Industry
& Agriculture
P.O. Box 208 Sharia Gamal Abdul Nasser,
Banghazi, Libya
Tel: (218) 95142

Mauritania Chamber of Commerce

Chambre de Commerce d'Agriculture et d'Industrie
de la Republique Islamique de Mauritanie
Boite Postale 215
Avenue de la Republique,

Nouakchott, Mauritania
Tel: (222) 52214/ 52215

Oman Chamber of Commerce

Oman Chamber of Commerce & Industry
P.O.Box 1400 Ruwi
Postal Code 112
Sultanate of Oman
Tel: (968) 707674/84/94
Fax: (968) 708497
Tx : (0498) 3389 ALGURFA ON
Cable: ALGURFA

Qatar Chamber of Commerce & Industry
P.O.Box 402,
Doha, Qatar
Tel: (974) 423677
Fax: (974) 324338
Tx : (0497) 4078 TIJARA DH

Saudi Arabia Chambers of commerce

Federation of GCC Chambers (FGCCC)
P.O. Box 2198
Dammam, Saudi Arabia 31451
Tel: (966) 3-8265943
Fax: (966) 3-8266794
Tx : (0495) 802176 FGC SJ

Council of Saudi Chambers of Commerce &
Industry
P.O. Box 16683
Riyadh, Saudi Arabia 11474
Tel: (966) 1-4053200/4057502
Fax: (966) 1-4024747
Tx : (0495) 405808 MAJLES SJ

Riyadh Chamber of Commerce & Industry
P.O.Box 596, Dabab St
Riyadh, Saudi Arabia 11421
Tel: (966) 1-4040044

Dammam Chamber of Commerce
Chairman: Sheikh Hamad Al Zamil
P.O.Box 719
Dammam, Saudi Arabia 31421
Tel: (966) 3-8571111/8571155
Fax: (966) 3-8570607
Tx :(0495) 801086 GHURFA SJ

Makkah Chamber of Commerce & Industry
P.O. Box 1086
Al Ghazza St.,
Makkah, Saudi Arabia
Tel: (966) 02-5343838/5342712
Fax: (966) 02-5342904
Tx : (0495) 540011 CHAMEC SJ

Jeddah Chamber of Commerce & Industry
P.O.Box 1264
King Khaled St, Ghurfa Bldg

Jeddah, Saudi Arabia 21431
Tel: (966) 02-6515111
Fax: (966) 02-6517373/6473026
Tx : (0495) 601069 GHURFA SJ

Somalia Chamber Of Commerce

Mogadishu Chamber of Commerce , Industry &
Agriculture
P.O.Box 27, Via Asha,
Mogadishu, Somalia
Tel: (252) 3209
Tx : (0900) 632

Sudan Chamber of Commerce
P.O. Box 81
Khartoum, Sudan
Tel: (249) 72346/76518

Syria Chambers of Commerce

Federation of Syrian Chambers of Commerce
P.O. Box 5909
Damascus, Syria
Tel: (0963-11) 3337344/3311504
Fax: (0963-11) 3331127
Tx : (0492) 411149 GOURAF SY
President: Dr. Rateb Shallah
Secretary General: Dr. AbdulRahman Attar
Damascus Chamber of Commerce
P.O. Box 1040
Mouawiah St, Harika Quarter,

Damascus, Syria
Tel: (963) 211339
Tx : (0492) 411326 GURFA SY

Aleppo Chamber of Commerce
P.O. Box 1262
El- Moutanabbi St.,
Aleppo, Syria
Tel: (963) 38236/7
Tx : (0492) 331012 ALICO SY

Damascus Governorate Chamber of Commerce
P.O. Box 5859
Damascus, Syria
Tel: (963) 339879
Tx : (0492) 412429 SY

Tunisia Chambers of Commerce

Union of Tunisian Chambers of Commerce &
Industry
103, Avenue De La Liberte, Tunis
1002 Belvedere Tunisie
Tunis, Tunisia
Tel: (0216) 1-780366/892457
Tx : (0409) 13982 UTICA TN

Chamber de Commerce de Tunis
P.O. Box 7943
6, Rue de Entrepreneurs,
Tunis, Tunisia
Tel: (0216) 1-242872/247669

United Arab Emirates Chambers of
Commerce

Federation of the UAE Chambers of Commerce &
Industry
P.O. Box 3014
Abu Dhabi, United Arab Emirates
Tel: (971) 2-214144
Fax: (971) 339210
Tx : (0893) 23883 GHURAF EM

Abu Dhabi Chamber of Commerce & Industry
P.O. Box 662
Abu Dhabi, United Arab Emirates
Tel: (971) 2-214000
Tx : (0893) 22449 TIJARA EM

Ajman Chamber of Commerce
P.O. Box 662
Ajman, United Arab Emirates
Tel: (971) 6-422177 Tx 69523

Dubai Chamber of Commerce &
Industry
President: Saeed Juma Al Naboodah
Director General: AbdulRahman G. Al Mutaiwee
P.O. Box 1457
Dubai, United Arab Emirates
Tel: (971-4) 280000
Fax: (971-4) 211646
Tx : (893) 45997 TJARA EM

Fujairah Chamber of Commerce & Industry
P.O. Box 738
Fujairah, United Arab Emirates
Tel: (971) 9-22400
Tx : (0893) 89077

Ras Al-Khaimah Chamber of Commerce &
Industry
P.O. Box 87
Al Sabah St.,
Ras Al-Khaimah, United Arab Emirates
Tel: (971) 7-33511
Tx : (0893) 99140

Sharjah Chamber of Commerce & Industry
P.O. Box 580
Sharjah, United Arab Emirates
Tel: (971-6) 541444
Fax: (971-6) 541119
Tx : (893) 68205 TIJARA EM

Umm Al Quwain Chamber of Commerce
P.O. Box 426
Umm Al quwain, United Arab Emirates
Tel: (971) 6-666915

Yemen Chambers of Commerce

Federation of Yemen Chambers of Commerce &
Industry
P.O. Box 16992

Hasaba, Airport Rd,
Sana'a, Yemen
Tel: (967) 2-232445
Fax: (967) 2-251551
Tx : (0895) 2229 YE

Sanaa Chamber of Commerce & Industry
P.O. Box 195, Sanaa
Hasaba, Airport Rd,
Republic of Yemen
Tel: (01) 232 361/232 362
Fax: (01) 232 412
Tx : (0895) 2629 YE

Hodeidah Chamber of Commerce & Industry
P.O. Box 3370
Liberty Square,
Hodeidah, Yemen
Tel: (967) 3-217401/217671
Fax: (967) 3-211528
Tx : (0805) 5610 GURFAH YE
Taiz Chamber of Commerce
P.O. Box 5029
Taiz, Yemen
Tel: (967) 4-210580
Fax: (967) 4-212335

National Chamber of Commerce & Industry
P.O. Box 473
Crater,
Aden, Yemen
Tel: (967) 51104/51203

Appendix L

National US-Arab Chamber of Commerce in the US

National Office
1100 New York Avenue, N.W.
East Tower, Suite 500
Washington, D.C. 20005
Tel: (202) 289-5920
Fax: (202) 289-5938

Branch Offices

208 S. LaSalle Street, #706
Chicago, IL 60604
Tel: (312) 782-0320
Fax: (312) 782-7379

420 Lexington Avenue, #2739
New York, NY 10170
Tel: (212) 986-8024
Fax: (212) 986-0216

1330 Post Oak Boulevard, #1600
Houston, TX 77056
Tel: (713) 963-4620
Fax: (713) 963-4609

Liaison Office
2711 LBJ Freeway, #122
Dallas, TX 77056
Tel: (214) 241-9992
Fax: (214) 241-0114

Affiliate Office
U.S. Arab Chamber of Commerce (Pacific) Inc.
P.O. Box 422218, San Francisco CA 94141-2218
Tel:(415)398-9200
Fax:(415)398-7111

World Chamber Of Commerce Directory
P.O.Box 1029
Loveland, CO 80539
USA
Tel: (970) 663-3231
Fax: (970) 663-6187

Appendix M

U.S. Department of Commerce - International Trade Administration District Offices

* ALABAMA

Medical Forum Building, 7th Floor
950 22nd Street North,
BIRMINGHAM, ALABAMA 35203
PHONE: (205) 731-1331
FAX: (205) 731-0076* ALASKA

Suite 319, World Trade Center Alaska
4201 Tudor Centre Drive,
ANCHORAGE, ALSKA 99508
PHONE: (907) 271-6237
FAX: (907) 271-6242* ARIZONA

Tower One, Suite 970
2901 N. Central Avenue,
PHOENIX, Arizona 85012
PHONE: (602) 640-2513
FAX: (602) 640-2518

*ARKANSAS

TCBY Tower Building, Suite 700
425 West Capitol Avenue,
LITTLE ROCK, Arknsas 72201
PHONE: (501) 324-5794
FAX: (501) 324-7380

* CALIFORNIA

11000 Wilshire Blvd., Room 9200,
LOS ANGELES, CA 90024
PHONE: (310) 235-7104
FAX: (310) 235-7220

3300 Irvine Avenue, Suite 305,
NEWPORT BEACH, CA 92660
PHONE: (714) 660-1688
FAX: (714) 660-8039

One World Trade Center, Ste. 1670,
LONG BEACH, CA 90831
PHONE: (310) 980-4551
FAX: (310) 980-4561
6363 Greenwich Drive, Suite 230,
SAN DIEGO, CA 92122
PHONE: (619) 557-5395
FAX: (619) 557-6176

250 Montgomery St., 14th Floor,
SAN FRANCISCO, CA 94104
PHONE: (415) 705-2300
FAX: (415) 705-2297

5201 Great American Pkwy., #456,
SANTA CLARA, CA 95054
PHONE: (408) 970-4610
FAX: (408) 970-4618

* COLORADO

1625 Broadway, Suite 680,
DENVER, CO 80202
PHONE: (303) 844-6622
FAX: (303) 844-5651

* CONNECTICUT
Room 610B, 450 Main Street,
HARTFORD, Connecticut 06103
PHONE: (203) 240-3530
FAX: (203) 240-3473

* FLORIDA

5600 Northwest 36th St., Ste. 617
MIAMI, FL 33166
PHONE: (305) 526-7425
FAX: (305) 526-7434

128 North Osceola Avenue,
CLEARWATER, FL 34615
PHONE: (813) 461-0011
FAX: (813) 449-2889

Eola Park Centre, Suite 695
200 E. Robinson Street,

ORLANDO, FL 32801
PHONE: (407) 648-6235
FAX: (407) 648-6756

107 West Gaines Street, Room 366G,
TALLAHASSEE, FL 32399
PHONE: (904) 488-6469
FAX: (904) 487-1407

* GEORGIA

Plaza Square North, Suite 310
4360 Chamblee Dunwoody Road,
ATLANTA, GA 30341
PHONE: (404) 452-9101
FAX: (404) 452-9105

120 Barnard Street, Room A-107,
SAVANNAH, GA 31401
PHONE: (912) 652-4204
FAX: (912) 652-4241

* HAWAII

P.O. Box 50026
300 Ala Moana Blvd., Room 4106,
 HONOLULU, Hawaii 96850
 PHONE: (808) 541-1782
 FAX: (808) 541-3435

* IDAHO

700 West State Street, 2nd Floor,
BOISE, Idaho 83720
PHONE: (208) 334-3857
FAX: (208) 334-2783

* ILLINOIS

Xerox Center 55 West Monroe Street, Suite 2440,
CHICAGO, IL 60603
PHONE: (312) 353-8040
FAX: (312) 353-8098

P.O. Box 1747
15 North Court Street,
ROCKFORD, IL 61110
PHONE: (815) 987-4347
FAX: (815) 987-8122

* INDIANA

Penwood One, Suite 106
11405 N. Pennsylvania Street
Carmel, IN 46032
PHONE: (317) 582-2300
FAX: (317) 582-2301

* IOWA

Room 817, Federal Building
210 Walnut Street,

DES MOINES, Iowa 50309
PHONE: (515) 284-4222
FAX: (515) 284-4021

* KANSAS

151 N. Volutsia,
WICHITA, Kansas 67214
PHONE: (316) 269-6160
FAX: (316) 683-7326

* KENTUCKY
601 W. Broadway, Room 636B ,
LOUISVILLE, Kentucky 40202
PHONE: (502) 582-5066
FAX: (502) 582-6573

* LOUISIANA

Hale Boggs Federal Building
501 Magazine Street, Room 1043,
NEW ORLEANS, Louisiana 70130
PHONE: (504) 589-6546
FAX: (504) 589-2337

* MAINE

187 State Street,
AUGUSTA, Maine 04333
PHONE: (207) 622-8249
FAX: (207) 626-9156

* MARYLAND

World Trade Center, Suite 2432
401 Pratt Street,
BALTIMORE, Maryland 21202
PHONE: (410) 962-4539
FAX: (410) 962-4529

* MASSACHUSETTS

164 Northern Avenue
World Trade Center, Suite 307,
BOSTON, Massachusetts 02210
PHONE: (617) 424-5950
FAX: (617) 424-5992

* MICHIGAN

1140 McNamara Building
477 Michigan Avenue,
DETROIT, Michigan 48226
PHONE: (313) 226-3650
FAX: (313) 226-3657

* MINNESOTA

108 Federal Building
110 South 4th Street,
MINNEAPOLIS, Minnesota 55401
PHONE: (612) 348-1638
FAX: (612) 348-1650

* MISSISSIPPI

201 W. Capitol Street, Suite 310,
JACKSON, Mississippi 3920
PHONE: (601) 965-4388
FAX: (601) 965-5386

* MISSOURI

8182 Maryland Avenue, Suite 303,
ST. LOUIS, Missouri 63105
PHONE: (314) 425-3302
FAX: (314) 425-3381

601 East 12th Street, Room 635,
KANSAS CITY, Missouri 64106
PHONE: (816) 426-3141
FAX: (816) 426-3140

* NEBRASKA
11335 "O" Street,
OMAHA, Nebraska 68137
PHONE: (402) 221-3664
FAX: (402) 221-3668

* NEVADA

1755 East Plumb Lane, Room 152
RENO, Nevada 89502
PHONE: (702) 784-5203
FAX: (702) 784-5343

* NEW HAMPSHIRE

601 Spaulding Turnpike, Suite 29,
PORTSMOUTH, New Hampshire 03801
PHONE: (603) 334-6074
FAX: (603) 334-6110

* NEW JERSEY

3131 Princeton Pike, Bldg. #6, Suite 100,
TRENTON, New Jersey 08648
PHONE: (609) 989-2100
FAX: (609) 989-2395

* NEW MEXICO

c/o New Mexico Dept. of Economic Development
1100 St. Francis Drive,
SANTA FE, New Mexico 87503
PHONE: (505) 827-0350
FAX: (505) 827-0263

* NEW YORK

1312 Federal Building
111 West Huron Street,

BUFFALO, NY 14202
PHONE: (716) 846-4191
FAX: (716) 846-5290

111 East Avenue, Suite 220,

ROCHESTER, NY 14604
PHONE: (716) 263-6480
FAX: (716) 325-6505

26 Federal Plaza, Room 3718,
NEW YORK, NY 10278
PHONE: (212) 264-0634
FAX: (212) 264-1356

* NORTH CAROLINA

400 West Market Street, Suite 400
GREENSBORO, NC 27401
PHONE: (910) 333-5345
FAX: (910) 333-5158

* OHIO

550 Main Street, Room 9504,
CINCINNATI, OH 45202
PHONE: (513) 684-2944
FAX: (513) 684-3200
Bank One Center
600 Superior Avenue, Suite 700
CLEVELAND, OH 44114
PHONE: (216) 522-4750
FAX: (216) 522-2235

* OKLAHOMA

6601 Broadway Extension, Rm. 200
OKLAHOMA CITY, OK 73116

PHONE: (405) 231-5302
FAX: (405) 231-4211
440 South Houston Street,
TULSA, OK 74127
PHONE: (918) 581-7650
FAX: (918) 581-2844

* OREGON

One World Trade Center, Suite 242
121 SW Salmon Street,
PORTLAND, OR 97204
PHONE: (503) 326-3001
FAX: (503) 326-6351

* PENNSYLVANIA

660 American Avenue, Suite 201
King of Prussia, PA 19406
PHONE: (610) 962-4980
FAX: (610) 962-4989

2002 Federal Building
1000 Liberty Avenue,
PITTSBURGH, PA 15222
PHONE: (412) 644-2850
FAX: (412) 644-4875

* PUERTO RICO

Room G-55, Federal Building, Chardon Avenue,
SAN JUAN, Puerto Rico 00918

PHONE: (809) 766-5555
FAX: (809) 766-5692

* RHODE ISLAND

7 Jackson Walkway,
PROVIDENCE, Rhode Island 02903
PHONE: (401) 528-5104
FAX: (401) 528-5067* SOUTH CAROLINA

Strom Thurmond Federal Bldg., Suite 172
1835 Assembly Street,
COLUMBIA, SC 29201
PHONE: (803) 765-5345
FAX: (803) 253-3614

* CHARLESTON

c/o Charleston Trident Chamber of Commerce
81 Mary Street,
COLUMBIA, Charleston 29402
PHONE: (803) 727-4051
FAX: (803) 727-4052

* SOUTH DAKOTA

200 N. Phillips Avenue, Commerce Center
Suite 302,
SIOUX FALLS, SD 57102
PHONE: (605) 330-4264
FAX: (605) 330-4266

* TENNESSEE

Parkway Towers, Suite 114
404 James Robertson Parkway,
NASHVILLE, Tennessee 37219
PHONE: (615) 736-5161
FAX: (615) 736-2454

22 North Front Street, Suite 200,
MEMPHISZIP, Tennessee 38103
PHONE: (901) 544-4137
FAX: (901) 575-3510

301 East Church Avenue,
KNOXVILLE, Tennesse 37915
PHONE: (615) 545-4637
FAX: (615) 523-2071

* TEXAS

P.O. Box 58130
2050 N. Stemmons Fwy., Suite 170,
DALLAS, TX 75258
PHONE: (214) 767-0542
FAX: (214) 767-8240

P.O. Box 12728
410 E. 5th Street, Suite 414-A,
AUSTINZIP, TX 78711
PHONE: (512) 482-5939
FAX: (512) 482-5940

#1 Allen Center, Suite 1160
500 Dallas,

HOUSTON, TX 77002
PHONE: (713) 229-2578
FAX: (713) 229-2203

* UTAH

324 S. State Street, Suite 105,
SALT LAKE CITY, Utah 84111
PHONE: (801) 524-5116
FAX: (801) 524-5886

* VERMONT

c/o Vermont Dept. of Economic Development
109 State Street,
MONTPELIER, Vermont 05609
PHONE: (802) 828-4508,
FAX: (802) 828-3258

* VIRGINIA

704 East Franklin Street, Suite 550,
RICHMOND, Virginia 23219
PHONE: (804) 771-2246
FAX: (804) 771-2390

* WASHINGTON

3131 Elliott Avenue, Suite 290,
SEATTLE, WA 98121
PHONE: (206) 553-5615
FAX: (206) 553-7253

* WEST VIRGINIA

405 Capitol Street, Suite 807,
CHARLESTON, West Virginia 25301
PHONE: (304) 347-5123
FAX: (304) 347-5408

* WISCONSIN

517 E. Wisconsin Avenue, Room 596,
MILWAUKEE, Wisconsin 53202
PHONE: (414) 297-3473
FAX: (414) 297-347

Appendix M

Arab Online Information Sources

http://www.arabamericanbusiness.com
http://www.arabmedia.com
http://www.arab.net
http://www.arab-business.net
http://www.arab-trade.com
http://www.arabdatanet.com
http://www.arabia.com
http://www.menow.com
http://www.mideastnet.com
http://www.nusacc.org
http://www.contactkuwait.com
http://www.kuwaitbook.com
http://www.kuwaitbusiness.net
http://www.kuwaitview.com
http://www.oman.org
http://www.omaninfo.com
http://www.directory-oman.com
http://www.omanyellowpages.com
http://www.timesofoman.com
http://www.mofa.gov.qa
http://www.arabji.com
http://www.qatartrade.org
http://www.qataryellowpages.com
http://www.qatarbusinesscouncil.org
http://www.saudiembassy.net
http://www.saudinf.com
http://www.saso.org

http://www.the-saudi.net
http://www.us-saudi-business.org
http://www.uae-pages.com
http://www.emirates.net.ae
http://www.emirates-online.de
http://www.kompass-uae.com
http://www.economy.gov.ae
http://www.uae.ac
http://www.uae-ypages.com
http://www.alqabas.com.kw/
http://www.alraialaam.com/
http://www.alwatan.com.kw/
http://www.arabtimesonline.com
http://www.kuwaittimes.net/
http://www.omandaily.com/
http://www.timesofoman.com/
http://www.raya.com/
http://www.al-sharq.com/
http://www.al-jazirah.com/
http://www.alriyadh-np.com/
http://www.arabnews.com/
http://www.saudigazette.com.sa/
http://www.alyaum.com/
http://www.albayan.co.ae
http://www.alittihad.co.ae/
http://www.khaleejtimes.co.ae/
http://www.yementimes.com/
http://www.yobserver.com/
http://www.akhbar-alkhaleej.com/
http://www.alwasatnews.com/
http://www.bahraintribune.com/
http://www.gulf-daily-news.com/

Appendix N

Online Trade Leads Sources

http://www.traderscity.com
http://www.enterprise.com.tw
http://www.afacerionline.com
http://www.allactiontrade.com
http://www.alleshandel.com
http://www.allproducts.com
http://www.tajernet.com
http://www.asiagoods.com
http://tradeinfo.asiannet.com
http://www.bisnis.doc.gov
http://www.bizviet.net
http://www.busytrade.com
http://www.chambertrade.com
http://www.china-exporter.net
http://www.chinapages.com
http://www.freetradefront.com
http://www.globaltradenetworks.com
http://trade.swissinfo.net
http://www.importers-exporters.com
http://trade.indiamart.com
http://www.indobiz.com
http://www.info-business.bg
http://www.tradezone.com
http://www.italbiz.com
http://www.jetc.com
http://www.marketz.com
http://www.marketz.com

http://www.mbendi.co.za
http://www.mblsales.com
http://www.mectrade.com
http://www.miriads.info
http://www.netglobaltrade.com
http://www.onetrade.biz
http://www.tenderseek.com
http://www.thaitradepoint.com
http://www.tradezone.com
http://www.tradeindia.com
http://www.trademmatch.co.uk
http://www.traderlisting.com
http://www.tradex-consulting.com
http://www.tramatch.com
http://www.venexport.com
http://www.wbdb.net
http://www.webindia.com
http://www.wholesalenet.com.au
http://www.wisben.com
http://www.wtexpo.com
http://www.worldtradeindex.com
http://www.wtpfed.org
http://world-trade-search.com
http://www.worldbid.com
http://www.worldtradeaa.com
http://www.ypage.com
http://www.yutrade.net

CPSIA information can be obtained
at www.ICGtesting.com
Printed in the USA
BVHW011443260421
605870BV00015B/417

9 780979 031113